Jealous for You

An Exposé of the Love of God

Brother Melvin

ISBN 978-1-64416-545-4 (paperback)
ISBN 978-1-64416-546-1 (digital)

Christian Faith Publishing
832 Park Avenue
Meadville, PA 16335
www.christianfaithpublishing.com

Printed in the United States of America

Contents

Synopsis

Jealous for You is a concise yet thorough look at the heart of God and his motives that would cause him to so love the world that he would give his only begotten Son to die for it. John 3:16 has been a verse of scripture used so flippantly in this day and age, that it is possible that the world has become immune to it, and God himself seems to be detached from it as well. However, it is the design of the thoughts in this survey of the love and person of God to put the attention back where it belongs, on God himself. From Genesis to Revelation, the complete thought of God about whom he is, who man is, and his revelation to man about his purpose is unveiled. In this presentation, we discover who is this God that declares that his name is Jealous? What are the key components that have aroused his jealousy to be expressed? Why is man so important to God that he would go to such an extreme to die on the cross of Calvary? What has God made known unto us about his feelings about his thoughts?

How should we examine and evaluate what he has said and done? What must we do with the things that he has made known? You should set your mind to be ready to see that which you may not have seen before and understand that which is not easily understood, as we discover why God is jealous for you.

The foundation of the thoughts of this idea of God being jealous for you is what God has said, "And God said, Let us make man in our image, after our likeness and let them have dominion" (Gen. 1:26a). The creation of man from God's perspective was good and his conclusion with his desire to make man in his image to be a representation of him on earth was very good. God's word is more to him than mere thoughts uttered out of his mouth. His word will not return unto him void, it will accomplish what he designed it to do. God designed that making the creature man in his image and likeness was intentional becoming his sovereign will and for his glory. However, because of sin, all that God had purpose for man and through man in creation was drastically destroyed. It had caused God to come to another conclusion that it had repented him that he made man because of the evil imaginations of his heart. Then God judged his creation and image that he had made was worthy of destruction. But God cannot lie; he must be true and faithful to his word. Although man failed and was not faithful by denying God, it is impossible for God to deny himself; he must be faithful to his word. God was in love with his work of creation, and it was evident that he was in love with man at first sight. It is imperative for us to understand that God is omniscient and had purposed before the foundation of the world to bring forth another man that would be the express image of his person that would do his will and manifest his glory. That person would be his word made flesh, his only begotten Son, the Lord Jesus Christ would rob man of his ability to obey and respond to God's love bringing him glory and honor, but God would restore all things through his Son. Let us first conclude what the jealousy of God is not. God is not afraid of losing something or so selfishly motivated that he has become bitter. He is not resentful of another's position, abilities, power, or intelligence. He is not full of envy because of something done to him by a rival or enemy, nor does he covet what someone else have, or think that they may be advantaged by. God is jealous for his image, his will, and his glory.

God has revealed some of his innermost thoughts and feelings about himself and his passion for his creation. In the pages of this book, we discover why is God mindfully of man? We consider, why is his image so important to him, and why is he offended at any and all misrepresentations of his person? God has revealed himself as, "El-Shaddai" the self-sufficient God. This thought about God is what we will explore to aid our understanding of his single-minded devotion. God saved man from himself, that is (from his wrath), God saved man by himself (he did everything), and he did it for himself, for his glory (that he may be just and the justifier of those that believe). We see the greatness of God his grandeur and glory in the expression of him humbling himself. Nothing less than a holy wonder and awe is to be exhibited at the thought of where God dwells in relationship to how he takes intimate notice of man. David observes these things with the utmost admiration for his Excellency manifested in this divine condescension toward man. God dwells in the highest heavens and in that realm, man is ignorant at best of its activity.

God has an exclusive right as God in all the things that he says and does. The thoughts and judgments of God are decisive and without question as he declares who he is and the immutability of his counsel.

God's exclusive right is based upon the absolute truth that he declares about himself, "I am God, and there is none else." There is no one or nothing that has an inherit right to loyalty or allegiance like God. Because of whom he is and what he has declared about himself, he validates the framework of his jealousy for his creation. There are things that God desire because of his person and purpose in creating man in his image. God has by design created the atmosphere for obedience to be complied with that in all things man may learn how to approach God, live before God, worship God, and serve God. Everything he required was to be done according to all that he said do. God never suggested or gave man the liberties to implement any of his thoughts pertaining to the things of God. God demands obedience in all things that he might make his presence known and manifest his glory. The jealousy of God is embedded in these components that are consistent with his person and his purpose.

God's love displayed covered all sins! Oh, how we need to grasp the depths of this truth and see who and how those that are guilty of sin, benefit from the display of this love. The disobedient, those who rebel against his word are considered free to come and haste themselves in this love and receive the richness of his mercy. God is jealous of the fact that man is blind and is like sheep without a shepherd in need of help to come into the knowledge of the truth about him. He has said that no man had seen God at any time. So he takes the responsibility very seriously to draw all men unto himself that they may have the opportunity to be saved and come into the knowledge of the truth. Jealous for you has brought together the simplicity and truth of the scriptures, with insights that God has made known about his person, to enlighten our understanding about the jealousy of God. His eyes go to and fro in the earth, and it is no secret that his love has been and is being rejected of men. But he is still committed to the word of truth. He is not willing that any should perish but that all men everywhere repent and be saved. The plan of redemption was a complete work of salvation involving the entire scope of the needs of God and man. We understand that God so loved the world that he gave his only begotten Son.

But it is the *what* and *how* of the plan that reveals the intricate details of this great salvation. This aspect of the work of God has been defined as a mystery because it has all been done in Christ. *Jealous for You* is a discovery of what is behind and involved in this manner of love.

What God purposed in his heart was to reconcile all things unto himself by the death, burial, and resurrection of Jesus Christ. Everlasting life is the will of God and has been from the creation of man. But here is the significant factor; God could not allow man to live forever in a sinful state, which is also the reason that Jesus took upon himself sinful flesh that he might take away the sin of the world. There is no religion, no ideology, no philosophy, and no self-made realization that could accomplish that. We all have an appointment with death no matter what culture, no matter what country, no matter what ideology, no matter what belief system. I submit to you three fundamental arguments about God for your consideration, ideological, practical, and spiritual. It has been determined that there are approximately 7.12 billion people on the face of the earth. That could also represent potentially the same amount of views or ideas about God. Some may say that it is relative what you consider to be true or false, right or wrong. We examine this thought with a higher regard for our lack of knowledge since we are so prone to be presumptuous. God has judged all of humanity as not being interested in him in sincerity and truth enough to seek to know him. Because of this lack of knowledge, he concludes also that there is none that understands the truth about him. It is a privilege to be able now to come into the knowledge of spiritual truth. No one has any rights or personal claims that they can magnify or justify to man or God about knowing what is spiritual truth. God has chosen by his grace and mercy to be willing to allow man to come into the knowledge of the truth on his terms alone. The God of faith has made himself known and the counsel of his will and that without reservation. He does not depend on or function because of the demands or assessments of men. How we view God affects every aspect of our life. What must this man do? *Respect.* In our conclusion, we present an acronym to validate what you must do that will not only certainly bring glory and honor to God but also bless you exceedingly, abundantly, above that which you could even ask or think.

Introduction

To those who do not know the Lord, there is a genuine concern about what they see and believe in regards to the Church, Christianity, and God. It has been said that Christianity means everything and at the same time nothing. It has been said that it does not make a difference what you believe; it is relative to who you are and your culture, and it is also a fact that many believe that there is no God. With all of these thoughts in mind, *Jealous for You* is a provocative look at the God of the Bible and his heart's desire according to scripture. The Bible has proclaimed that God so loved the world that he gave his only begotten Son, that whosoever believes in him should not perish but have everlasting life. *Jealous for You* is a concise look at who is this God and why would he do this? And what does it really mean? There are over seven billion people on the face of the earth, and everyone has their own thoughts and views about God. *Jealous for You* brings this reality to bear as it examines the heart of God toward his creation. The Bible is clear on the truth that in conveys—no man hath seen God at any time! Therefore, it is God's responsibility and his alone to make known who he is and how he chooses to reveal himself.

When God created man in his image, this meant more to him than we normally perceive. Man was to be the representation of the person of the Only True and Living God on earth. As we survey the scripture, we will find that God's commitment to his word will supersede all other things for he has magnified his word above his name. God is jealous for his image, his will, and his glory; this will be the foundation of this presentation of how we will discover that God is jealous for you. The creation of man was the act of the sovereign will of God, the image of God and his likeness that was manifested in man was destroyed by sin. This offense to a Holy God would deprive him of making known his glory in his creation as he intended. God could not allow his word to return unto him void by not accomplishing what he purposed. Therefore, because of him being God alone in his Omniscience, Omnipresence, and Omnipotence, he purposed before the foundation of the world to correct the problem. Since man was the object of his love, he would validate his concern for the misrepresentation of his image by sending his Son.

Jealous for You examines some of the clear thoughts that God has revealed about his feelings concerning the work of his hands. It unveils his exclusive rights as God and his claims to his creation. In the beginning, God created, God established, and God executed his will by the authority of his word. It is the authority of his word that has been under attack from works of the devil to the disobedience of man. The truth of the matter will always prevail. Heaven and earth will pass away, but his word endures forever. *Jealous for You* will provoke you to place your attention on the God of the Bible like never before as he makes known some of the intents of his heart. Never before has man been able to approach the invisible God, but now he can see clearly his innermost thoughts. Prepare your hearts and minds to be ravished with his love and raptured by his single-minded devotion. The cross of Calvary was an unimaginable expression of the jealousy of God expressing itself with unreasonable love. It can be denied, but it can never be undone.

It is impossible for God to lie, so he worked a wonderful work of grace by making his word become flesh, so that we could behold his glory. The Word of God being made flesh would be the expressed image of his person that would reconcile all things that God intended. Remember it was God, who said, "Let us make man in our image, and in our likeness." God is a jealous God, and in the pages of this book, you will witness the beauty of his glory and the purpose of his will in sending his Son to die on the cross to take away the sin of the world. There is nothing that can compare to the redemptive work of the cross of Calvary, and in it, God validates his love for his creation and justifies why he is jealous for you. The fear of the Lord is the beginning of the knowledge of God. God is jealous for you to the extent that he has done everything necessary for you to come into the knowledge of the truth. He admonishes you to ask and it shall be given, seek and you shall find, knock and the door shall be open to you. As we conclude the thoughts of this book, we challenge you to consider the need to *respect* what God has done, why he has done it, but most importantly, who he is.

1

Love at First Sight

So God created man in his image, in the image of
God created he him; male and
female created he them.
And God saw everything that he
had made, and behold,
It was very good.

—Genesis 1:27, 31a (KJV)

It is very probable that everyone has placed a high value on their affections, especially when it is in regards to our relationships. However, we determine who we choose to devote our affections toward. It is reasonable to assume that we have concluded it to be very good. Throughout the history of humanity, love has been a desire that everyone has truly longed for. We have applauded love stories that provoke our desires for love as they have helped formulate our understanding of love's presence and the effects of its absence. *Romeo and Juliet* was an example of young love taunted by family disapproval exemplifying tragedy and loss. *Casablanca* depicted a long loss heartache fueled with passion rekindled, and *The Hunchback of Notre Dame* conveyed through Esmeralda how love faced with the distasteful and deformed could cause one to conclude that "love is like a tree; it grows by itself, roots itself deeply in our being and continues to flourish over our hearts in ruin." The inexplicable fact is that the blinder it is, the more tenacious it is. It is never stronger than when it is completely unreasonable. "We can see a vivid similarity in God's unreasonable love for us as we search with earnest intent the scriptures. Yes, God's love for us exceeds the bounds of reason. His love is excessive in its demands, absolute about its claims, and expressive with purposeful passion. It is more completely unreasonable to conceive since he spared not his own Son, who died for our sins to prove it. Our failure to rightly appreciate the magnitude of so great a love is why we need to understand how and why God is jealous for us. I do not claim to compare our understanding of being jealous in a negative context in relation to God being jealous for us. Neither is this an attempt to belittle the person and redemptive work of the Lord Jesus Christ. However, in simplicity and truth, this is provocative look at God's passion for his thought, his will, and the work of his hands.

We have always looked at the fact that "God so loved the world that he gave his only begotten Son". But behind the action is a wonderful and amazing reality of why it meant so much to him personally. This is where we will explore the depths of God's character revealed in the scriptures to look afresh at the love of God. The Creator of the universe and all things therein has woven throughout scripture an intimate look at his heart. It is my desire to present a clear accounting of God being a jealous God for his most prized creation—"man". One most important discovery that will enable us to understand this similarity is taking a close look at how God has valued his image. What did God mean when he said, "Let us make man in our image, after our likeness" (Gen. 1:26a, KJV), and what did it mean to him to see it done? Let's examine the image of God from his perspective to help us build on this idea. What is an image? An image is a representation or similitude of a person formed. Man, being created in the image of God, would display the communicable attributes of God. It has always been God's desire to reflect how he is in and through man from the beginning that he might put himself on display. This is where "our image" and "our likeness" holds the most value to God.

The Omnipotent, Omniscient, Omnipresent, True and Living God determined within in himself, for himself and by himself to reveal himself to and through his creation. Man would become the perfect expression of himself bodily on earth. That being said, it builds a clear platform for us to see how he attaches so much of his person to man being made in his likeness and his image. The scriptures declare that no man hath seen God at any time (John 1:18, KJV). Therefore, it is incumbent upon God himself to not only to reveal himself, but also to define how he has made himself known. And the Lord God formed man of the dust of the ground and breathed into his nostrils the breath of life; and man became a living soul (Gen. 2:7, KJV). Likewise, and the Lord God caused a deep sleep to fall upon Adam, and he slept; and he took one of his ribs, and closed up the flesh instead thereof; And the rib, which the Lord God had taken from man, made he a woman, and brought her unto the man (Gen. 2:21–22). Humanity has been given the most marvelous and wonderful place in the scheme of God's creative purpose. Only man was designed by God putting his hands upon him to form how he would be. All other creatures were created by God speaking them into existence, but man was different; he was formed by the hands of God. This personal touch represented an intimate and passionate expression of God's handiwork, making man into his likeness and his image. Let's look further into the characteristics of "the image and likeness of God." After the physical formation of man, the scriptures declare that God "breathe into his nostrils the breath of life." This not only made man a living soul, but it also imparted unto man a spiritual nature that enabled him to communicate with and worship God. God is a Spirit, and they that worship him must worship him in spirit and in truth (John 4:24, KJV). Man was not only self-conscious, he became God conscious. His communion with God was a byproduct of his being created in the image of God and in his likeness.

Being in his likeness, we were given personality to further manifest the person of God. He is personable, and this identification with him made it possible for us to have individual diversity while being able to relate with one another through are emotions, intellect, and behavior. Our will, intellect, and emotions are primary faculties given to us that express the image of God. They enable us to develop and express his likeness. The nature of man was blessed with the privilege to choose. This inept right has been defined as having the ability to decide, determine, and demonstrate of one's own volition. It is interesting to note that when God created man, he obligated him to make decisions freely.

And the Lord God commanded the man, saying, of every tree of the garden thou mays *freely* eat; But of the tree of the knowledge of good and evil, thou shalt not eat of it (Gen. 2:16–17a, KJV) in the likeness of God, man could purpose within himself to act upon his desires and interest. However, being subject to the Sovereignty of God, he was given a command that required the choice of obedience to please God. Man's obedience would be an expression of righteousness, bringing glory and honor to God exemplifying his image and likeness. For it was the will of God to see man honor him by reflecting simple childlike obedience to the utterance of his command. God gave him the free will to choose to obey at the same time be aware of the reality of disobedience. It is very unfortunate that we have, over the years of human history, failed to place the high value that God has placed on obedience. Obedience was and is to God the highest expression of love toward God that can be expressed. Obedience affects the heart, mind, will, and emotions causing complete and whole relationship between God and his creation. Obedience fuels the revelation of the glory of God manifested in man, for even the winds and the sea obey him. Obedience is the expression of perfection that reflects the holiness of God in man because we are one with him.

It is impossible for us in our natural mind to grasp the beauty and power that was designed in obedience, because disobedience was the original choice and the sin that deprived man of experiencing that glory. Therefore, as we continue along this discourse, it is imperative to keep in mind that to see things from God's perspective, you must have the right mind-set. The apostle Paul wrote:

And you hath he quickened, who were dead
in trespasses and sins; Wherein in time past ye
walked according to the course of this world,
according to the prince of the power of the
air, the spirit that now worked in the children
of disobedience: Among whom also we all had
our conversation in times past in the lusts of our
flesh, fulfilling the desires of the flesh and the
mind; and were by nature the children of wrath,
even as others. (Eph. 2:1–3, KJV)

Another component in man being made in the likeness of God
was that he was given intelligence. Having the capacity to perceive
knowledge with understanding separated man from all other creatures that were created. Adam had intuitive knowledge and understanding that enabled him to name all of the animals. He also would
be able to continually learn and appropriate knowledge as one of the
attributes that was bestowed upon man being made in the image of
God; "God himself being the God of all knowledge and understanding." The misuse of knowledge has proven to be one of the greatest temptations of man. It was the knowledge of good and evil that
tempted man in the beginning and knowledge misappropriated has
continually been man's demise. The scriptures paint a perfect picture
of all things being placed in its order. If knowledge is misappropriated it becomes true that "knowledge puffed up."

We have heard the saying, "knowledge is power," this is to suggest that the more that you know, the more ability that you have to
execute and accomplish thought and actions, rather they be good or
evil. We have also heard the statement that, "the mind is a terrible
thing to waste," understanding that to allow ourselves to be dormant
and not develop the potential of our ability through the learning
and understanding process could be detrimental. On both sides of
the spectrum, we are vulnerable; to one extreme, being ignorant of
knowledge leads to all manner of evil, likewise being full of knowledge in excess can lead unto all manner of evil. It is no coincidence
that the Proverb writer places the fear of the Lord before knowl-

19

edge. The fear of the Lord is the beginning of knowledge (Prov. 1:7a, KJV). God has determined that man need to have a sense of respect and admiration for the capacity to learn and know knowledge, especially sense his capacity has so much potential being made in the image of the God of all knowledge. This gives us even more reason to appreciate why God would limit man's access to the knowledge of good and evil. Every aspect of man being made in the likeness and image of God had significance to God himself being able to put him on display in the earth. Another aspect of man being made in the likeness of God was the expression of emotions. Literally, a moving of the mind or soul; hence, any agitation of mind or excitement of sensibility. God has revealed himself to be willing and able to express the depth of his feelings through emotional display. Throughout the scriptures, God depicts his expressions of love, mercy, peace, joy, and even anger wherein appropriate. Thus for man to do likewise is consistent with man being made in his likeness. These are just a few brief examples to bring some clarity toward understanding how man is made in the image and likeness of God. These observations do not attempt to define the depth of God's perspective of making man in his image and likeness, but it gives us a good foundation to validate how and why he would be jealous for his creation. Seeing that it is his image and likeness that was intended to be put on display. "Thou art worthy, O Lord, to receive glory and honor and power: for thou hast created all things, and for thy pleasure they are and were created" (Rev. 4:11, KJV). If we can behold the desire of God in all of his beauty and splendor being pleased with his creation that he created for his pleasure, it will be easy to see how he would not want anything to take it away from him, or deprive him of the liberty to enjoy it.

Using these thoughts as a basic understanding of what is meant by being made in the image and likeness of God, let us attempt to grasp why God was committed to love at first sight. He had observed the works of his hands and beheld his glory that was bestowed upon man and concluded that it was "very good". The image of his person has now been physically manifested, and his joy is exemplified in the fact that humanity is an expression of him on earth. Male and female made he them! This was truly an expression of God not only manifesting his image and likeness but also the ultimate expression was highlighted in man's ability to reproduce life. We cannot begin to imagine what was in the mind of God when he took Adam and Eve placed them in the garden of Eden naked and innocent. The word *Eden* itself literally means "delight". Be fruitful and multiply, and fill the earth with life. The imagery of Eden is beyond our comprehension. Can you see it? Every tree pleasant to the sight, and good for food, a river so vast that comes out of Eden it splits into four heads and speaks of lands with gold, bdellium and onyx stones. Oh! How wonderful, Oh! How marvelous, we should really be struck with awe! Finally, man is given authority to rule, govern, and manage the work of God because he is so pleased with his creation that it was love at first sight. David gives us some insight into how God's affection for the creation of man was so dear to him.

> What is man that you take thought of him, and the son of man that thou visitest him? For thou hast made him a little lower than the angels, and hast crowned him with glory and honor. Thou maddest him to have dominion over the works of thy hands; thou hast put all things under his feet. (Ps. 8:4–6, KJV)

Man is given an exalted place in the creation of God because of God's affection and pleasure in him. He looks upon man and sees the glory of himself and is overwhelmed with love and joy. Nothing can compare to this love at first sight for man is created in innocence. When life is first birthed and we see it with our own eyes, we intuitively commit our love and affections without reservation because we see it as very good. How precious it is to behold the glory of our own reproduction and can we not see God doing the same? It is true that God is not like man, but it is also equally true that God made man in his image and likeness. His word will not return unto him void. He said, "It is very good." This was his conclusion, his will and the work of his hands.

2

<hr />

Robbed of Affection

And thou shalt love the LORD *thy*
God with all thine heart,
And with all thine soul and with all thy might.

—Deuteronomy 6:5 (KJV)

To attempt to describe how much it means to a Holy God to be loved is beyond man's capacity to comprehend or even effectively communicate. However, we can get a glimpse of the heart of God and his desire to be loved in this amazing truth revealed in his word. To understand how God has been robbed of affection, we must recognize his need for it. The "Great Commandment" gives us some insight into these things as we discover its purpose. Let's examine closely what is involved in the whole idea of this commandment. We clearly see in it the object of this love is God himself. Why would God command that we love him? God is not like man in that his needs are similar to ours. God is by his very nature perfect needing nothing. His need to be loved by us is for his glory and our good. It is no wonder for us to consider that if we are infused by a spirit of love, ruled by a passion to love, and devoted to a life of love, to expect to be loved in return. However, this is not the picture that the Bible conveys to us about the True and Living God. The scriptures conclude that God is love. The very essence and embodiment of love is defined in knowing who

God is. Why would God command man to love him? I think that this deserves our attention with fear and trembling because it could be so easily misunderstood. There are three dynamics mentioned in the expression of this commandment to love. To love God with all thine heart. It is no secret what God has concluded about the heart. "The heart is deceitful above all things, and desperately wicked: who can know it?" (Jer. 17:9, KJV). This truth presents a major problem for man and his ability to comply with God's command.

How can one express such love from a heart so defiled and unfit to appropriate it? How can one even desire such a love being ruled by a heart that is full of deceit and wickedness? Just consider how God felt when he decided to judge the earth with the flood.

> And God saw that the wickedness of man was great in the earth, and that *every imagination of the thoughts of his heart was only evil continually*. And it repented the Lord that he had made man on the earth, and it grieved him at his heart. (Gen. 6:5–6, KJV; emphasis mine)

This is a devastating indictment toward man, but it also reveals the depth of God's hurt to see what sin has done to his image. In the previous chapter, we discussed how God was so pleased with his creation of man to the extent that he concluded it to be very good. A well-balanced expression of his image and likeness. Now he is so grieved that there is such a gross misrepresentation of his person that he wished he never made man. Rather we believe it or not God destroyed mankind and all of his creation by the flood because his image and likeness was so distorted that he could not look upon it. Sin had driven man to such a vulgar state of degradation that it repented him to his heart. His holiness, honor, image, and likeness have been deliberately injured. The only remedy for this tragedy was a new heart.

> A new heart also will I give you, and a new spirit will I put within you: and I will take away

the stony heart out of your flesh, and I will give you a heart of flesh and I will put my spirit within you, and cause you to walk in my statutes, and ye shall keep my judgments, and do them. (Ezek. 36:26–27, KJV)

Second, to love the Lord with all the soul. We have come to understand the soul to be the seat of all our desires. Can you imagine God wanting you to desire him above all things? No, you can't. It is impossible to phantom such a thought because sin has caused us to have a reprobate mind. Our disposition is at enmity with God; we hate God. God would have us to seek him with the whole heart diligently, but we do not seek at all. David wrote, "Delight thyself also in the Lord: and he shall give thee the desires of thine heart" (Ps. 37:4, KJV). I am convinced that David was making a clear reference to his desire for God with all his soul and thus he became a man after God's own heart. Lastly, this command challenges us to love the Lord with all our might. Are you kidding me? This could be considered an obsession with God. If we could only get a glimpse of the depth of the relationship that God desires with us, we would understand why God wrote:

And these words, which I command thee this day, shall be in thine heart: And thou shalt teach them diligently unto thy children and shalt talk of them when thou sittest in thine house, and when thou walkest by the way, and when thou liest down, and when thou rises up. And thou shalt bind them for a sign upon thine hand, and they shall be as frontlets between thine eyes. And thou shalt write them upon the posts of thy house and on thy gates. (Deut. 6:6–9, KJV)

The effort and energy that God has suggested we show toward him is unparalleled to anything. He commands that we seek him first, he describes how we should seek him diligently and with all withholding nothing.

We read in the book of Revelation "Thou art worthy, O Lord, to receive glory and honor and power: for thou hast created all things, and for thy pleasure they are and were created" (Rev. 4:11). How can we approach these things without first having a good foundation to build upon? Consider for a moment, what would make one worthy? To be valued as one who possess worth that would qualify distinguishing merit. We could conclude immediately that God is deserving of our love in the fact that he alone created us. Many would argue that there is no God, or that creation was the result of a big bang that evolved into this amazing and unique thing that we have come to know as life. The importance, value, and excellence that is associated with the idea that there is a True and Living God gives him worth. God is, and he is willing to make himself known to his creation in such a fashion that they can become intimate with him. Something this marvelous and wonderful could only be describe as exceedingly, abundantly above what we could ask or think. The fact of the reality of sin and the damage that it wrought in the earth and upon God's creation has caused our hearts to become foolish and full of darkness. Leaving us hopelessly crippled and unable to respond to God with the glory and honor that he deserves, therefore, robbing him of affection. The nature of God has an inherent majesty that could be defined as his glory. It is a reflection of his divine presence, power, majesty, and honor. His glory has more to do with his reputation as the Only True and Living God and a manifestation of his excellence. When man was created for his pleasure and glory God was revealing a perception of himself that displayed his moral beauty. This was the ground that man would begin to relate and conduct himself toward God and man. Man by his virtue was designed to conform and comply with divine law, thus glorifying God. Man as a creature would prescribe the honor and respect due toward his Creator. This would validate the affection that man had for God showing his willful reasoning and actions that resulted in obedience However, it is imperative that we understand that it was the act of *disobedience* that dishonored God. This would become the thief that would rob God of his affection and set man on course of a path toward hating God and all that he represents. It is unfortunate that many fail to come to a place of understanding about the state and nature of sin. The word of God has made it perfectly clear that "for as by one man's disobedience, many were made sinners" (Rom. 5:19). It is sin that deceived man and destroyed his ability to show any affection toward God. The sin of disobedience carried with it eternal damage to the order of God and would prove to be the source of man's bondage. To help us evaluate the character and damage of this great sin, we need to consider its consequences.

> And the Lord God commanded the man, saying, of every tree of the garden thou mays freely eat: But of the tree of the knowledge of good and evil, thou shalt not eat of it: for in the day that thou neatest thereof *thou shalt surely die*. (Gen. 2:16–17; emphasis mine)

First of all, for man to disobey God willfully placed him under God's judgment of immediate death. This was God's righteous judgment for an offense against his nature, character, and holiness. God by his very nature is Sovereign. He is the only absolute authority. There is no other God! He answers to no one, needs no approval from any, and who alone is Omnipotent, the character of God is light, and in him is no darkness at all. Disobedience plunged man into the power and bondage of darkness separating him from all fellowship with God. Finally, this sin of disobedience was a direct insult to the Holiness of God. He is set apart from all other things made, seen and unseen, exhibiting his infinite pureness and perfection. We can only imagine in a glimpse a Holy God, because holiness is beyond our comprehension. "Holy, holy, holy, LORD GOD ALMIGHTY, which was, and is, and is to come. The damage that disobedience inflicted upon a Holy God can only be concluded as evil. How has this tragedy affected the Creator? The scriptures declare, "For God so loved the world that he gave his only begotten Son, that whosoever believeth in him shall not perish, but have everlasting life" (John

3:16). Truly, God's heart was broken over the fact that what he had created was subject to death. He could not stand by and do nothing. He purposed within himself to save his creation for his glory. He recognized that there was nothing man could do for himself to deliver himself from this deprived state. But God, who is rich in mercy, for his great love wherewith he loved us, sent forth his son to die for our sins. Herein is love, not that we loved God but that he loved us, and sent his Son to be the propitiation for our sins (1 John 4:10). The implications of God not sparing his own Son to secure an opportunity to love us passes all understanding. "For scarcely for a righteous man will one die: peradventure for a good man some would even dare to die? But God commended his love toward us, in that, while we were yet sinners, Christ died for us" (Rom. 5:7–8). We also see evidence throughout scriptures of God expressing his forbearance, long-suffering, and forgiveness to validate his faithfulness and love. These are not the actions of one who is expecting love but one who is proving love.

When we examine the original sin of disobedience, we can clearly see how God was robbed of affection. Satan as a thief came to steal, kill, and destroy. By lying to Eve in the beginning, he stole the desire to please God from her by tempting her to please herself. Questioning what God had said, "Yea, hath God said; ye shall not eat of every tree of the garden?" Satan knew that God said that if they were to disobey and eat the fruit, in that day, they would "surely die". He also knew that it was impossible for God to lie. "And the serpent said unto the woman, ye shall not surely die: For God cloth know that in the day ye eat thereof, then your eyes shall be opened and ye shall be as gods, knowing good and evil" (Gen. 3:4–5). Yielding to the temptation, she became subject to the desire to please herself. The desires to please ourselves always kill any affection toward God and destroy our ability to obey him. Therefore, it was imperative for God to give such a command to love the Lord thy God with all thine heart, and with all thine soul, and with all thy might. Although the command was designed for our good, it was impossible for us to completely obey it. This command would reveal our inability to please God and propel us to cleave to Jesus as our saving hope. For what God intended to be accomplished in Adam was fulfilled in Jesus Christ the second Adam. This is my beloved Son in whom I am well pleased! We see how the apostle Paul manifested the character of God's love when he wrote: "And I will very glad spend and be spent for you; though the more abundantly I love you, the less I beloved" (2 Cor. 12:15). He exemplified the love he spoke of that suffered long and is kind: love envied not; love vaunted not itself, is not puffed up. "Doth not behave itself unseemly, seeketh not her own, is not easily provoked, thinketh no evil: rejoiced not in iniquity, but rejoiced in the truth; Beareth all things, believeth all things, hoped all things, endured all things." Love never failed (1 Cor. 12:4–8a). A love so defined and descriptive as this can easily be understood as willing to go to whatever extreme necessary to secure the object of its love. We could never underestimate the extremes that one would go to not only prove their love, but also to protect that love through their jealous passion of the one that they love being hindered from receiving that love or deprived in any way from knowing the reality of it. Nothing can be more devastating than to have someone who you love to believe something about you that are not true, have no resemblance of truth, and cause such misunderstanding that it becomes irreconcilable. The enmity that sin caused between God and man was formulated on those grounds. God had no knowledge of sin, and it is the very corporate that deprived God of become intimate with the creature that he decided to make in his image. Nothing could be as devastating to God as to have to separate himself from the creation that he designed for his glory in order to prevent it from being destroyed. Sin cannot survive in the presence of the True and Living God because of his holiness. In the greatness of his power and by his matchless wisdom, he took on sinful flesh to touch with the infirmities of man, but also to show his jealousy for his image, his will, and his glory that was made known we he said, "Let us make man in our image, and in our likeness." This is the manifestation of the beauty of the Lord wherein he so loved the world that he gave his only begotten Son.

3

---◆((◉))◆---

The Jealousy of God

For thou shalt worship no other god: For the LORD,
Whose name is Jealous, is a jealous God.

—Exodus 34:14

We must approach this particular subject matter with fear and trembling, for this is on "Holy Ground." One of the most challenging aspects to our understanding of the character of God is the fact that he is Holy. Our limited capacity to grasp even the reality of Holiness is so far removed from its truth that it leaves us ignorant. However, this is a small yet inadequate attempt to examine the awesomeness of this truth, as it relates to the jealousy of God. It is recorded in the scriptures that God commanded Moses to approach him in a specific way because of his holiness. "And he said, draw not nigh hither: put off thy shoes from off thy feet, for the place whereon thou staidest is holy ground" (Exod. 3:5, KJV). The Spirit of God is the only one who can reveal not only who he is but also how he is. Considering this fact, let's examine what God was revealing about himself to Moses in this particular incident. God makes it clear to Moses first of all that his presence is like none other. He is Holy, and because of this fact alone, he can only be approached with high regards to his holiness, lest you die. He is God alone, and there is no other God. He instructs Moses on how to approach him with full attention toward his complete explicit obedience. He charges Moses to take his shoes from of his feet because his presence has made even the ground Holy. There must be a preparation of mind and will as we consider approaching God, for he is not of this world. It is no secret that his ways our not our ways, and his thoughts are higher than our thoughts. Therefore, we have need of instruction to be led in the way of understanding the jealousy of God. Let us first conclude what the jealousy of God is not. God is not afraid of losing something or so selfishly motivated that he has become bitter. He is not resentful of another's position, abilities, power, or intelligence. He is not full of envy because of something done to him by a rival or enemy, nor does he covet what someone else have, or think that they may be advantaged by.

Cain killed his brother Abel because he was jealous of his gift being accepted before God and his rejected. This negative connotation and image of jealousy is far from the jealousy of God because these things are rooted in evil distrust, strife, and hatred. We have all experienced the reality of jealousy as it manifest itself as the works of the flesh, full of threatening and rage. But God is not like man, neither can he be confined to the finite constraints placed upon the creature, for he is the Creator. God does not consider the remotest thought of anyone or anything being compared unto himself.

> To whom then will ye liken me, or shall I be equal? saith the Holy One. Lift up your eyes on high, and behold who hath created these things, that bringeth out their host by number: he calleth them all by names, by the greatness of his power: for that he is strong in power: not one faileth. (Isa. 40:25–26, KJV)

The character of God in reference to being jealous is motivated by his intentions and zeal. When we investigate godly jealousy, as it relates to God, we can clearly see that it is impossible for God's love and sensual jealousy to coexist. His selfless love was exemplified in seeking the highest good for his creation. There has never been a time wherein God seeks to see what he can get out of something only how he can display his glory.

When God instituted marriage, he was revealing something about himself since he made man and woman in his image. He was revealing covenant relationship by the two marrying and becoming one. It was to be a divine and holy institution magnifying his person and expressing his glory. The scriptures often reflect on God's love toward the children of Israel as his bride and the ultimate consummation of Christ and his bride the church. Herein is the atmosphere created for the jealousy of God as he commits himself to covenant relationship. In Exodus 34:14, the theme verse we are using to convey the jealousy of God, it highlights several elements to help us understand the jealousy of God. The first element that I would like us to examine is the idea of worship as it relates to the Only Wise God. Worship in itself reveals to us the reverence, admiration, adoration, high esteem, and awe that convey him having the Preeminence. Nothing can negate the fact that there is no other God, not our ignorance, our unbelief, or our imagination. He is the only Potentate, the only one worthy of all glory, honor and praise. "O worship the LORD in the beauty of holiness: fear before him, all the earth" (Ps. 96:9). He alone is set apart, he alone is high and lifted up, he alone is God. God has made known to us that no one and nothing is to be placed above him in our hearts, mind, and life. The sad reality is that we have done just the opposite. We have intentionally worshipped the creature more than the Creator, allowed our affections to be wholly given to other things that eventually become our gods. We serve them with all our strength, all of our mind, and all of our heart. Things such as sports, exercise, money, prestige, desire for power, knowledge, and accomplishments, even our children, houses, cars, own thoughts and imaginations. But God will not share his glory with another or allow the flesh to glory in his presence. These thoughts become very relevant as we uncover the jealousy of God. God is jealousy of his honor, his glory, and his image. God, by his very nature, will protect those things that are preserved by his covenant relationship and be armed and ready to judge any and all threats that attempt to injure or provoke. As we move forward in this discovery, let's keep in mind that the things that God has made known unto us about himself are for us.

In this covenant relationship that God has established for his name sake, he likens himself as a faithful husband committed to love and honor. His honor is devoted to his wife and their relationship. Just as he charged Adam in the beginning. "Therefore shall a man leave his father and mother; and shall cleave unto his wife: and they shall be one flesh" (Gen. 2:24, KJV). It is his will that we cleave unto him for our life. God desires a pure relationship that creates an intimate oneness with his person. Nothing and no one can disturb, deprive, or make demands against it. He arms himself ready to take vengeance on any and all that threatens to bring dishonor to his name, for in his name is his reputation and identity made known. His glory is manifested in his name as his will is done on earth as it is in heaven. The glory of God warrants him being intentional where he chooses to reveal himself. He puts himself on display in the things that he has designed that represent his person and image. Therefore, in this covenant relationship, God expects his creature to respond to his mercy and grace therein. Remember that God created man for his pleasure and glory. In his covenant, he gave promises, commands, and instituted warnings for our good and protection thus justifying his claims on his creation for his honor, glory, and image. Promises to assure man of the comforts, benefits, and pleasures that compliment being in covenant relationship. It is amazing grace at its best bestowed upon man, showering him with blessings exceedingly, abundantly, above all that he could ask or think. God promises his goodness, mercy, loving-kindness, providence, favor, and even eternal life through this covenant relationship. This becomes the lifeline of resourcefulness that frames the characteristics for his jealousy. Moses experienced the glory and holiness of God and has conveyed to us valuable insight to help our understanding.

> And the LORD passed by before him, and
> proclaimed, The Lord GOD, merciful and gra-
> cious, long-suffering, and abundant in goodness
> and truth, Keeping mercy for thousands, for-

giving iniquity and transgressions and sin, and that will by no means clear the guilty; visiting the iniquity of the fathers upon the children, and upon the children's children, unto the third and to the fourth generation. (Exod. 34:6–7, KJV)

The jealousy of God is just and sure because of whom he is as God alone in covenant relation to *his creation*.

His name is Jealous because his image is Holy! There is a beauty like none other manifested in knowing the True and Living God. This knowing that he declares is an experiential knowing that brings man into oneness with his holiness, oneness with truth, oneness with light, and oneness with life and that more abundantly. As I stated earlier in this chapter that this is but an attempt to present only a mere glimpse at an aspect of the person of God that can easily be perceived as beyond our understanding. The jealousy of God is embedded in his holiness, which is breathtaking. The scripture paint an awesome picture in the heavens about God that we in our finite state on earth are far removed from. The imagery could be described as unbelievable in its essence. However, in the spirit of truth, it uncovers for us the unsearchable riches of which he is and how he has made himself known. This is their testimony: And the four beasts had each of them six wings about him; and they were full of eyes within: and rest not day and night, saying Holy, holy, holy, LORD GOD Almighty, which was, and is, and is to come (Rev. 4:6, KJV). If you can only imagine but for a moment that this proclamation of adoration of God's holiness does not cease. This should capture our attention to the fact that we do not really see him as he is. God is jealous for his image, his will, and his glory. He will not allow his eyes to be satisfied with the distorted damage that sin has done to his image that he had created of himself in man. Therefore, he sent forth his Son made in the express mage of his person to redeem man from that state for his own name sake.

His will on earth was not fully realized because of the presence of sin. Therefore, he purposed in his heart to reestablish his will on earth. "The next day John seeth Jesus coming unto him, and saith,

Behold the Lamb of God, which taketh away the sin of the world" (John 1:29, KJV); thus preparing the way for God to fulfill his will with a new heaven and new earth because of it. Now we are able to behold his glory for has glorified himself in his Son Jesus Christ through the death, burial, and resurrection. He can glorify himself in man by delivering him from the bondage of sin and death, placing him in Christ creating a new creation. God will not share his glory with another. He alone is worthy of all the glory, so he has an inherit right to make known to his creation that he is a Jealous God. He works out of his jealousy toward his best interest in man, his will, and his glory. Jesus prayed, "I have glorified thee on the earth: I have finished the work which thou gavest me to do. And now, O Father, glorify thou me with thine own self with the glory which I had with thee before the world was" (John 17:4–5, KJV). The glory of God is a manifestation of his magnificence, his beauty, his splendor, his majesty, his greatness and the greatness of person, his presence, and his praise. Any inclination of misrepresentation of who he is, what he has done, or how he has made himself known provokes him in his holiness to jealousy. For he has said that his name is Jealous should he not respond out of his nature to be true to himself and all the things which concerns him, his character, and his name.

4

The Object of His Love

What is man, that thou art mindful of him?
And the son of man, that thou visitest him?

—Psalm 8:4 (KJV)

What value has God put on man knowing that he is a rebellious sinner destined to hell and destruction to manifest his righteous judgment? Why would a Holy God invest so much of his affection in someone who hate and despise everything he represents? How could man be so important to God that he would even send his only begotten Son to die in his place? These questions are baffling when you consider some of the assessments the scriptures has made concerning man. We noted earlier that God said, "He saw that the wickedness of man was great in the earth, and that every imagination of the thoughts of his heart was only evil continually" (Gen. 6:5, KJV). It is inconceivable for us to know the depth of the offense to a Holy God to look upon such evil. Can you imagine what it would take for God to witness man being defiled and defiling each other in his presence? There is no fear of God, no regard for his person or will. There is no consciousness of God's honor, no concerns about being made in his image, no idea about or identification with the glory of God. Living with all manner of wicked behavior and imaginations that it provoked him to destroy man from off the face of the earth. Just to get it into your mind, this view of man is not our view.

It is rather easy for us to conclude that man is not that bad. However, confident we may be about our thoughts, our thoughts are not God's thoughts. Let's consider further what the scriptures say about man. "They are all gone aside, they are all together become filthy; there is none that doeth good, no, not one" (Ps. 14:3, KJV). The last time I checked, all meant literally everyone. This indictment upon man is all inclusive; no one is exempt from it. What needs to be understood is that all of humanity and every aspect of life are deprived of God. Man is so self-willed and stubborn that all of his actions and thoughts are toward his own desires, ambitions, and indulgences. None of his thoughts are toward God, none of his interest is in the things of God, and neither is his decisions influenced by God. As much as we would want to conclude, it is not an accurate description that we would own up to, it is in fact an absolute truth. This indictment not only includes how we are but also what we do. The conclusion is that because of sin and our sinfulness, we can do nothing that is of any good value from God's perspective. Our actions are defiled because we are. We are likened to those that are plagued with leprosy; they are defiled and everything they touch becomes defiled.

We are prone to think higher of ourselves than we ought, and this makes it impossible for us to see ourselves as God does without his grace. The reality of sin has to be acknowledged and accepted for what it is and the damage it has done. Our lack of understanding of the damage that sin has done is really the issue. "For sin, taking occasion by the commandment, deceived me, and by it slew me" (Rom. 7:11, KJV). Man is spiritually dead and destined to physical death of which all must eventually face. Herein is why man is the object of God's love. God created man in his image for his glory, and it was not his sovereign will for man to die. He now looks upon man in his fallen state helpless, hopeless, and compelled by his own mercy to act. His mercy rises within him to the occasion to show forth his loving-kindness. There is a massive difference between what God intended and what we have come to experience as a result of sin.

We will never be able to reenact what the original design and plan of God for man was. However, because it was his plan, it is within him to recall and act upon his purposes. It was God's purpose to make man in his image and likeness. It was God's purpose to manifest his glory on the earth through man and all that he created. Therefore, he is more than able to revise, revisit, and reconsider how to fulfill his purposes. In the beginning, God concluded that what he had created was very good, and as it is written, his word will not return unto him void. God must make good on his word for it is impossible for him to lie. Man is the object of his love primarily because he is made in the image and likeness of God. David asked the question, "What is man that thou art mindful of him?" In order for God to fulfill his purpose for man, he had to address the problem that man created. Man has found himself in a position under the judgment of God separated from his person, fellowship, and without excuse in this world. Since God had executed the sentence of death upon all, for all had sinned and fall short of the glory of God. His righteous judgment needed to be satisfied. The only way that man could satisfy the judgment of God would be to die. This was the only option that would make things right in the eyes of God. Then there was the whole issue of the existence of sin. Sin, by very nature, must be totally taken out of the situation so that God can reenter and have a relationship with man and enjoy his fellowship. There was no way that these things could happen without man. In this instance, we must consider the importance of the human nature of man to participate and help God execute his purpose toward man the creature created in his image. The first Adam has placed the purpose and glory in disarray and yet it is also the Adamic nature that is necessary to aid in its own deliverance.

At this point in our discovery, I would like to redirect your attention to God. "And he saw that there was no man, and wondered that there was no intercessor: therefore, his arm brought salvation unto him; and his righteousness, it sustained him" (Isa. 59:16, KJV). In this scripture reference, we see God's thoughts toward man and his need to have an intercessor. The need for someone who would come into his situation and represent him by identifying with his state and needs. He also conveys his need for someone to take part and making it possible for man to be saved because he saw that there was no man to help. God's continuous love and affection for man in his low estate is evident throughout scripture. God chooses to make himself known as the Redeemer of mankind so that he can be glorified in being just and the justifier of man. God has by his loving-kindness implemented a great plan of redemption for man. No other creature has been given the privilege and experience of such mercy and grace with so much emphasis on being redeemed. This salvation is spoken of as being so great that the angels desire to look into it. Man has been given a place of glory in honor in the scheme of God's handiwork that he has been personally involved with every aspect of his redemption. As we move forward, let us now consider how God in his matchless wisdom begins to bring to light his thoughts. The second part of the question that David asked that we must answer is, "And the son of man that thou visitest him?" The God of heaven and earth and all things that therein are, desires and expresses genuine interest in man that he is willing to visit with him. This is no mere visitation but an expression of interest in his person, concern about his thoughts, and willingness to fellowship with him. Man is the object of his love. He has proven with many infallible proofs his love, which literally passeth understanding. If we could but catch a glimpse of his thoughts toward us, we would never be the same.

What can we learn about this idea of God visiting the son of man? What was involved in the process of this thought? We have come to understand that Adam not only represents God's first thought about making man in his image, he also represents that which is made of the flesh. The flesh is where we need to focus our attention as we begin to look at God creating another man. This creation was unique in that it was born of a woman who was a virgin. It is interesting to consider what God did in preparing another body of flesh so that he could be faithful to his word and himself. This is not an attempt to play down the significance of the virgin birth; rather, it is an attempt to look at the process for insight into the heart of God concerning his thoughts toward his creation, man. But let's look at something that is worthy of our attention when it comes to the body of flesh. In the New Testament, we find this recorded:

"Wherefore when he cometh into the world, he saith, Sacrifice and offering thou wouldest not, but a body hast thou prepared for me" (Heb. 10:5, KJV). This is the revelation of the body of flesh that is to be considered the second Adam. Another human nature that would be perfectly fit to accomplish the whole and complete will of God as man. This man is the God-Man! Absolutely 100 percent, God manifest in the flesh and 100 percent the flesh of man. The apostle Paul describe it on this wise, "And without controversy great is the mystery of godliness: God was manifest in the flesh, justified in the Spirit, seen of angels, preached unto the Gentiles, believed on in the world, received up into glory" (1 Tim. 3:16, KJV). We should stand amazed that God would take it upon himself to be cloth with flesh to identify with humanity for the sole purpose of delivering him from sin and death that he might magnify his word. Why would I say that he might magnify his word? If we will consider the writing of the apostle John, he said, "In the beginning was the Word, and the Word was with God, and the Word was God. And the Word was made flesh, and dwelt among us, (and we beheld his glory, the glory as of the only begotten of the Father,) full of grace and truth" (John 1:1, 14, KJV). We can only conclude here that God thought it to be the only way to accomplish what he originally purposed in man being made in his image. He spoke his word into the Virgin Mary and conceived a body of flesh that manifest him and complete what he initiated in making man in his image. Furthermore, the writer of Hebrews gives us even a clearer picture of the truth about this new God-Man, "Who being the brightness of his glory, and the express image of his person" (Heb. 1:3a, KJV). Notice here how he is not just made in his image he is the express image of his person. He would be the new human nature made of flesh fitted to take the judgment of sin and death for all of humanity. Yet at the same time filled with the fullness of the Godhead bodily able to make peace with God and place in man the image that pleased God. I would also boldly proclaim here that the Omniscience, Omnipotent God Almighty purposed this also before the foundation of the world. We will explore more of this subject in forthcoming chapters.

And so it is written, the first Adam was made a living soul; the last Adam was made a quickening spirit (1 Cor. 15:45, KJV). The Bible does make a distinguishing observation about the first and last Adam. Let us not be deceived here the first Adam as we have search out and discovered was responsible for bringing upon all men sin and death. The second Adam who is Jesus Christ because of his death, burial, and resurrection has paid our sin debt in full by satisfying God's judgment of death. But because he was God incarnate, death was not able to hold him and on the third day, he rose from the grave according to the scriptures and was given all power in heaven and earth. Thus enabling him also to give life to whosoever believes and set their hope in him. This is the amazing grace of God expressed in him dealing with the truth and fact of sin as well as the power of God to do the impossible. The things which are impossible with men are possible with God (Luke 18:27, KJV). Allow me to provoke your thoughts by asking you to consider a pop song written by Joan Osbourne. The title of her song was "What If God Was One of Us". In her song, however critical or controversial it may have been to many, she makes some observations that I think we can examine and ask some legitimate questions. She states in her lyrics if God had a face, what would it look like? This question suggests the possibility of God being flesh and blood and leads one to consider several ideas that she conveys. Could he look like a slob like one of us? Could he just be another stranger that we randomly pass by in the course of a day? Interestingly enough, God was so mindful of man that when he took on flesh, he visited man as a baby born in a manger. He grew up as the son of a carpenter. He was considered the sinner's friend associating with the despised, rejected, and sinners from all walks of life. Finally, he was crucified being accused of being a liar and deceiver. God was one of us the scriptures declares:

> For verily he took not on him the nature of angels; but he took on him the seed of Abraham. Wherefore in all things it behooved him to be made like unto his brethren, that he might be a merciful and faithful high priest in things per-

taining to God, to make reconciliation for the
sins of the people. (Heb. 2:16–17, KJV)

Hopefully, some of these thoughts will cause you to consider
investigating further the claims of Christ. What is man that thou
art mindful of him? Man is the only creature that God created and
honored him to be made in his image and likeness. Man is the only
creature that God created that was given dominion over the works
of his hand on the earth. Man is the only creature that God himself
took on flesh to become an intercessor for. Man is the only creature
that God so loved the world that he gave his only begotten Son to die
for. There is no greater truth with as much eternal value as this. Man
is the object of his love, and it is not because we love him. For when
we were without strength in due time Christ died for the ungodly.
"For scarcely for a righteous man will one die: yet peradventure for a
good man some would even dare to die. But God commendeth his
love toward us, in that, while we were yet sinners, Christ died for us"
(Rom. 5:6–8, KJV). The first Adam was destined to death; the second Adam died to give eternal life. The first man produced the spirit
of disobedience; the second God-man brought unto us the spirit of
obedience. The first Adam was earthly minded; the second Adam
heavenly minded. As we continue to unfold the riches of his grace in
examining how God has made himself known, we will see him in the
scriptures as the lover of our souls. If we were to consider the imagery
that God has revealed in the Love "Song of Songs" that he wrote, we
could easily conclude that there is no greater lover than the God of
love. He pursues with a passion and protects with a valor that likens
him to a man of war. His love is self-sacrificing and provocative, not
to be compared to any other, and more to be desired than life itself.
So let him draw you unto himself and let his kiss you with the kisses
of his lips and be forever raptured by his love.

5

Why Is God Jealous for You?

And the spirit lifted me up between
the earth and the heaven,
And brought me in the visions of
God to Jerusalem, to the door
of the inner gate that looketh toward
the North: where was the seat
of the image of jealousy, which
provoked unto jealousy.

—Ezekiel 8:3b (KJV)

In order for us to have any reasonable understanding of why God is jealous for you, there must be the realization that this is a spiritual matter. The scriptures have declared plainly that we wrestle not against flesh and blood, but against principalities, against the rulers of the darkness of this world, against spiritual wickedness in high places (Eph. 6:12, KJV). In this chapter, we will begin to get at the root of problem that God has that has stirred up his jealousy for man throughout the ages. That which is flesh is flesh and that which is spirit is spirit. These are the things that concern God the most because they are that which brings the most offense to his person. It is an affront to God to display in his face anything that would attempt to claim more allegiance to or take away from the conscience of man, God. Remember, we have already determined beforehand that man was created for God's glory and pleasure was he created. It is the principalities, rulers of darkness in this world, and spiritual wickedness that is not seen with the natural eye that continually steals, cheats, and destroys man and his ability to respond to God aright that provokes him to such jealousy because man is his creation. Man is taken captive and those of us given the responsibility seek for the souls of men have been charged with a serious mandate.

> And the servant of the Lord must not strive;
> but be gentle unto all men, apt to teach, patient,
> In meekness instructing those that oppose them-
> selves; if God peradventure will give them repen-
> tance to the acknowledging of the truth; And
> that they may recover themselves out of the snare
> of the devil, who are taken captive by him at his
> will. (2 Tim. 3:24–26, KJV)

We will never be able to grasp an understanding of God that will make us above reproach, but God has made known somethings about his person that should keep us humble before him. God had declared that his name is Jealous, and it is necessary for us to approach this truth with a discerning spirit. His name is not just a title for recognition, but his name carries with it the depth of who he is and all he represents. Let's first consider what is in a name? When we consider the Most High God, his name alone conveys his character who he is and what he is like. It reveals his reputation and history with all that he has said and done. This could be the very reason why it is written, "Thou shalt not take the name of the LORD thy God in vain; for the LORD will not hold him guiltless that takes his name in vain" (Exod. 20:7, KJV). The attack on the True and Living God is above and beyond our finite ability to really identify with. This is a vicious attack that started by Satan himself and continues to this day to provoke the jealousy of God. In the beginning, Satan accused God of lying and being a liar. He proclaimed to Eve by his very actions that what he was saying was true and should be believed above and beyond that which God has said. I say these things in fear and trembling as just the thought of them are dangerous to even consider. To call the Only True and Living God a liar when it is impossible for him to lie.

The attacks that provoke the jealousy of God is anything and everything that suggest that there is another God, or bring into question what God has said accusing him to be a liar, or even questioning the very existence of God. These attacks are the very atmosphere that spiritual wickedness and rulers of darkness attempt to distort the truth about God. Unfortunately, man is the vulnerable victim in all things that pertain unto God.

> Because that which may be known of God is manifest in them; for God hath shewed it unto them. For the invisible things of him from the creation of the world are clearly seen, being understood by the things that are made, even the eternal power and Godhead; so that they are without excuse: Because that, they knew God, they glorified him not as God, neither were thankful; but became vain in their imaginations, and their foolish heart was darkened. (Rom. 1:19–21, KJV)

Man has become so prone to using the name of God with reproach and contempt that even their consciences have become seared. But God who is rich in mercy remember his name that he has placed on man being made in his image. God remembers that it is his glory and honor that is at stake and his jealousy rises to the occasion to not only protect his name but also to protect his image and glory. Much damage has been done in the mind and hearts of men as their view of God has been confused and entangled into a web of uncertainty and disbelief. The very thought of the devil taking men captive at his will is surely a sign of how defenseless and vulnerable man is.

In the verses that we are using to open this discussion, Ezekiel is caught up into a vision to observe things from God's perspective.

Israel was guilty of idolatry in the temple of God. Nothing provokes God to jealousy more than giving his worship, glory, and honor to another. We can learn from the admonition of scripture that God finds these things as an abomination to him. How can a creature that he has created and prescribe to worship him only be so easily deceived into thinking that there is another worthy of praise and worship? Satan and all the rulers of darkness have preyed on the ignorance and vulnerability of man throughout the ages. Even the people of God have become victim to the crafty cunning works of the enemy.

> And no marvel; for Satan himself is transformed into an angel of light. Therefore it is no great thing if his ministers also be transformed as the ministers of righteousness; whose end shall be according to their works. (2 Cor. 11:14–15, KJV)

The reality of spiritual warfare has been misperceived on a large scale seeing that many are not only ignorant of his devices but also biblically illiterates. God has made himself known throughout the scriptures in his relationship with those specific men that he has chosen as well as his relationship with the children of Israel. However, it has been the primary objective of Satan and all the forces of darkness to prevent man from coming to know the truth. Jesus spoke expressively about this matter when he said, "Ye are of your father the devil, and the Inst of your father ye will do. He was a murderer from the beginning, and abode not in the truth, because there is no truth in him. When he speaketh a lie, he speaketh of his own: for he is a liar, and the father of it" (John 8:44, KJV). This is another reason why God is jealous of man, because he "who will have all men to be saved, and to come unto the knowledge of the truth" (1 Tim. 24, KJV) sees man in bondage of darkness.

God is a God of Light and in him is no darkness at all. When God created man in his image, it was the will of God that man would be a light barer to the world displaying the Father of lights. He did not change his desire because John spoke of Jesus testifying of the same truth, "In him was life; and the life was the light of men. And the light shineth in darkness; and the darkness comprehended it not. That was the true Light, which lighted every man that cometh into the world" (John 1:4–5, 9, KJV). The essence of God is the most important thing to be considering as we look at all that he has done in creation. Everything that he has done is a representation of his name and image. The fact that he has been provoked to jealousy should been viewed with a high regard for his person with respect. It is a sad testimony about man that our view of God has been so distorted, that we cannot even appreciate the fact that God's being and very essence has been degraded, and it has provoked him to jealousy. God is jealous for you because you do not know the truth about him. God is jealous for you because you are like a sheep to blind, frail, and defenseless to do anything about it. God is jealous for you because you are taken captive by the enemy at his will. God is jealous for you because it is he that has created you and not you yourselves. God is jealous for you because it is his nature to protect and defend his name, image, glory, and honor. God is jealous for you because you are the only visible creature that has any resemblance of the invisible God. God is jealous for you because for his glory was you created. God is jealous for you for he hath said, "Let us make man in our image and our likeness." Man is his creation, if we could but identify with his passion for his thought, his desire, his will, we will see with undeniable clarity that he is just in his affections. From man's perspective with no input of his own, it is great and greatly to be praised that God would make man in his image and in his likeness. This honor and majestic favor is unparalleled to all other creations, creatures, heavens, stars, mountains, or even the seas. God is jealous for you because he is great and his greatness is unsearchable!

6

No Greater Love

*Greater love hath no man than this, that a man
lay down his life for his friends.*

—John 15:13 (KJV)

Of all the things that are to be understood, God's love is the only
thing that is beyond our understanding. The love of God has been
clearly defined and without any contradiction has been exemplified yet it requires a greater understanding than our finite minds
can grasp. Paul wrote that we, "May be able to comprehend with all
saints what is the breadth, and length, and depth, and height; And
to know the love of Christ, which passeth knowledge, that ye might
be filled with all the fullness of God" (Eph. 3:18–19, KJV). But our
knowing it and experiencing it is not the same as understanding it.
In this chapter, it is my desire for us to examine the greatness of
this love. How can we even measure the greatness of it since there
is nothing to compare it to? Love is a subject that we are limited in
our depth of experience and understanding; however, it is one of our
greatest needs. Our relationships are often off balanced because of a
misperception of our expectations of love. We often find ourselves
enjoying the benefits of being loved but fall short when it comes to
meeting the demands of love. The different aspects of love that we are
familiar with only touch the surface of the essence of love. We know

and appreciate the romantic love that leads to intimacy that only last but a moment. We can never belittle the love we have experienced as children of parents that bestowed upon us affection that will last a lifetime. But how much pain we have borne when we realized that out love was limited and expired. How much disappointment we knew as we saw our children whom we loved so much choose to love things we forbid them not. Love as we know it has provided for us joy and pain.

Love has also been a word we use to describe some of anything that blows across our emotions. We love everything from ice cream to football as long as it is bringing the self-satisfaction that we crave from it. This is one of the reasons that we are so uncertain about the essence and true character of love. Too often, we see love as something we can turn on and off like a light switch with no idea of its quality. I say these things only to help enlarge your view of what we have come to associate the word love with in our day to day life experiences. But from God's perspective, love takes a radical turn and elevates all that we could ever ask or think about it. If the truth be told, we had not known anything about true love until the LORD himself has come to make it known. With that being said, let's seek and discover some of the amazing truths about this love that Jesus is declaring in which there is nothing greater than. A love so great that it is greater than any and all aspects of love that we have ever imagined. Love so great that it could probably be considered unsearchable. Although God has given us many wonderful truths in the scriptures to examine his love for us, we still miss the mark when it comes to realizing the greatness of it. David wrote, "Great is the LORD and greatly to be praised; and his greatness is unsearchable" (Ps. 145:3, KJV). What can we gather from this thought about being great? Great in the sense that it is awe-inspiring, magnificent, and significant. Great by means of being majestic, eminent, and dominant. This great God in all his greatness has manifested a great work of love for the whole world to come and experience.

It is no secret that the Bible records a continual theme that man is faced with throughout history and that is his unbelief. Man's failure to believe God has been a tragedy that he has lived with from one generation to the next. One of the main causes of man's failure to not only experience this love but to even acknowledge its existence is unbelief. We can only imagine someone loving us enough to die for us as a remote possibility in certain circumstances. Maybe a parent willing to die for a child whom they see facing a very present danger. We may even find a chivalrous husband willing to die for his wife in face of the shadow of death. But the scriptures have declared, "For scarcely for a righteous man will one die; Yet peradventure for a good man some would even dare to die. But God commendeth his love toward us, in that while we were yet sinners, Christ died for us" (Rom. 5:7–8, KJV). No one in their right mind naturally speaking would even consider dying for someone that the do not know. It may be probable in a given situation in the perils of war that bravery may lead one to sacrifice their life in the spirit of gallantry and valor. However, when we really consider the truth about valuing someone else life more than our own, it is at best a remote possibility. Our very nature is to be self-conscious and self-preserving. There are three observations I think you should look at to help you get a glimpse of the greatness of this love. First, God commended his love! He gave a charge to his love to execute toward man. God knowing the inexhaustible riches of his love commanded love to move and act in the fullness of its power. He commendeth his love to show his righteousness, mercy, and justice. He bestowed great grace, great mercy, and great deliverance for a great need that man had. He commissioned his love like an armed solider going into battle to secure the victory over all enemies. The charge was to cover the multitude of sin, comfort with everlasting comfort, and renew a right spirit within man by purging all of his sin. The charge was for love to prove and establish the occasion to stand for and with fallen man to uphold him with his power. To intercede in his behalf until complete satisfaction is secured for the glory of God to be manifested in man, making peace with the Most High God. He charged his love to provide holy acceptance and continuing forbearance and forgiveness that man might be empowered to become the sons of God. He charged his love to establish an eternal covenant relationship written in blood that would speak volumes throughout eternity. He commanded that love would be the law to govern all the affairs of man and rule with its principles everlasting life. This charge of love would be summoned unto complete obedience even unto death.

A dying love that we might live and have life more abundantly was the result of this commission. It was great in that it was an open display of a profound self-sacrificial love. It was great proclaiming the A forgiveness of sins forever. No one is unreachable under the broad scope of this eternal love pursuing to the uttermost realms of sins destruction. Second, this act of selfless love was toward those who had no merits for it, those gone astray and without any regards for God. It was great in enduring all the shame and offense that would come against the holy nature of God with only one expectation. The only expectation of this great love was the joy of seeing those that were on the receiving end of it benefit from its effects. God himself has taken the initiative with sufficient motive to deliver and make man a part of his eternal family rewarding himself only with the joy of seeing it done. This is great and truly the greatness of it is unsearchable. "For he hath made him to be sin for us, who knew no sin that we might be made the righteousness of God" (2 Cor. 5:21, KJV). The greatness of this action demands our attention. We will do ourselves well when we come to understand and identify with the fact of the reality of sin and the fact of the atonement. Great was the damage of sin to man but even greater was the fact that the atonement was able to satisfy the penalty of it. It is more than wonderful, more than marvelous to know, that Christ has paid the penalty of our sin to make us the righteousness of God. Mere words cannot express the magnitude of the atoning, substitutionary work of the Lord Jesus Christ. His representation of man and sin for the sole purpose of being reconciled to God is great and greatly to be praised. Let us not be slow in our understanding as we observe this fact and intentionally think upon it to value its significance. Jesus said that there is no expression of love that compares to such as this. No love has ever met the criteria of loves that looks beyond the faults of men, covers them, and then make them right in his own eyes. This is a great work of the hands of God to plant all mankind in Christ that he might taste death for every man and impart righteousness to every man. Our view of God should be enlarged as he entreats us with his favor and draws us with his loving-kindness. This is love that pass our understanding, love that provokes us to receive the grace of God. This love compels us to submit to his divine judgment and cleave to him for our life. God's view of us is overshadowed by this great love, forgiving all of our past, present and future sins and making us accepted in Christ. We did not choose him he chooses us and showers us with the multitude of his blessings. It is sad to think that our harden hearts and unbelief do prevent us from responding to him as we ought. "But God who is rich in mercy for his great love wherewith he loved us, Even when we were dead in sins, hath quickened us together with Christ, by grace are ye saved" (Eph. 2:4–5, KJV),

Third and most important, "Christ died for us." This is the truth that is the key that sets all men free. The truth, the whole truth and nothing but the truth. Death is the judgment of God on man because of sin, but it has also become the deliverance for man because of Jesus Christ. We cannot think for a moment that the death of Jesus did not happen. We cannot make his death to be just a common thing as if it was a normal occurrence. His death was intentional and it was intentional for you personally. This personal identification supersedes all of our thoughts, feelings, and imaginations. Christ dying for us suggests that there was a purpose that had an objective in mind.

> But we see Jesus, who was made a little lower than the angels for the suffering of death, crowed with glory and honor, that he by the grace of God should taste death for every man… For as much then as the children are partakers of flesh and blood, he also himself likewise took part of the same; that through death he might destroy him that had the power of death, that is the devil; and deliver them who through fear of death were all their lifetime subject to bondage. (Heb. 2:9, 14–15, KJV)

Very little is said today about the devil being destroyed, but the death of Christ's primary objective was to destroy the devil. It was the devil that deceived Eve and set the course of man in the direction of destruction. It was the devil that is the father of lies, a thief and a murderer from the beginning. Let's be clear here the devil has led all men captive at will and continues to this day to seek to devour. The death of Christ was the greatest victory for man in the history of humanity. Yes, there is no greater love than this! God is not in the business of doing things in vain or for no intended purpose. God has a plan and will that he will execute on earth as it is in heaven. A crucial part of that plan was and is the redemption of man. God has made himself known to us in such a fashion that he desires to call us friends. When Jesus said that this great love is expressed only by the laying down of his life, this should let us know the standard of God is great. Isaiah gives us some insight into the heart of God when he wrote, "Come now, let us reason together, saith the LORD: though your sins be as scarlet, they shall be white as snow; though they be like crimson, they shall be as wool" (Isa. 1:18, KJV). God is exhibiting here the riches of his mercy to show man how reasonable he is in considering their state and their need. He calls us to come boldly to him to find the grace and mercy to meet us at our point of need. All of our needs may vary but the one common need that we all have is him. We need him to deliver us from our sin, we need him to open the eyes of our understanding, and we need him to help our unbelief. As much as it seems reasonable to you come and reason with me he proclaims. I am the one who is touched with all of your infirmities; I am the one who knows how frail you are. This is another example of how great the love of God is toward us in that he is willing to meet us on common ground as a wonderful counselor. Again, we are compelled to consider the great work that was accomplished at the cross of Calvary. The atonement meets every need and satisfied the righteous judgment of God, now he is able to freely give.

When we hear the word *friend*, we can honestly say that we normally have types. We have those friends by association, that being those that we see and who seeing us because we associate at work, church, or some other activity. We also have friends that we know by their name, we can identify with who they are and to some degree how they are. Then we have those intimate friends and they are far and few in between. But please take heed with the utmost care the thought that the God of heaven and earth. The only True and Living God, who through giving his only begotten Son to die for our sins desires to call us friends. The Scriptures teach us that Enoch walked with God and was not; also that Abraham was called the friend of God. What a privilege that so few have come to enjoy, and so many know nothing about. Just consider for a moment how great it would be to know God in such closeness that he considers you a friend. This is an honor that many do not even desire because they are ignorant of him. This love is so great that God even went farther than that, a Paul wrote, "What shall we then say to these things? If God be for us, who can be against us? He that spared not his own Son, but delivered him up for us all, how shall he not with him also freely give us all things?" (Rom. 8:31–32, KJV). There is nothing to compare to the greatness of God's love for us. There is no one who has proven such love with many infallible proofs. There is no one out of the reach of his all-inclusive love for all. These are but a few reasons to validate that there is no greater love than this that has ever existed or that will ever exist. Therefore, we would be wise to hasten unto him; we would be wise to call upon him while he is near. In the classic gospel hymn "What a friend we have in Jesus", there is a stanza that states, "Oh what peace we often forfeit, oh what needless pain we hear, all because we do not carry everything to God in prayer." There are some friends that come and go in life, but there is one who will be with you forever. God is a personal God, who is touched with all of our infirmities, and acquainted with all of our thoughts. Always willing to show the goodness of his mercy to all that look unto him in sincerity and truth. He is so willing to prove the love that he has toward his creation; however, no one can begin to grasp the magnitude of this love but those who by faith respond to it and enter into this covenant relationship of fellowship with the Father and the Son. But as it is written, "Eye hath not seen, nor ear heard, neither have entered into the heart of man, the things which God hath prepared for them that love him" (1 Cor. 2:9). The Spirit of God speaks expressively through his word, making them known only to those that turn unto him and receive his instruction.

7

God's Single-Minded Devotion

*For this is good and acceptable in the sight
of God our Savior: Who will have all men to saved,
and to come unto the knowledge of the truth.*

—1 Timothy 2:3–4

Many things could be said about being devoted to a cause, a person or a goal. But coming into the knowledge of the truth is worth comparing nothing. God has command his love to reclaim that which was lost to him through the fall of man. Now that the work is finished he has set his face toward pursuing man that they would be saved from his wrath. God has revealed himself as, "El-Shaddai" the self-sufficient God. This thought about God is what we will explore to aid our understanding of his single-minded devotion. God saved man from himself, that is (from his wrath), God saved man by himself (he did everything), and he did it for himself, for his glory (that he may be just and the justifier of those that believe). The handiwork of God is exemplified from Genesis to Revelation providing for us an opportunity to witness his majestic masterpiece, the redemption of man. As we examine how God has made his thoughts known, we will come to identify with his single-minded devotion. How do we define single-minded? Single-minded has to do with a determined and concentrated commitment to one specific purpose. There is no room for alternative or distracted interruptions because the focus is steadfast and resolute. When we consider what devotion entails, we can conclude that a display of love and loyalty with high regards and interest would be applicable. God's provision for man's redemption came at a great cost and for that reason, the value that God has placed on salvation is priceless. At the transfiguration of the Lord Jesus Christ, we see the single-minded devotion of God initiated,

> While he yet spake, behold, a bright cloud overshadowed them: and behold a voice out of the cloud, which said, This is my beloved Son, in whom I am well pleased; hear ye him. And when the disciples heard it, they fell on their face, and were sore afraid. (Matt. 17:5–6, KJV)

The testimony that God has given his only begotten Son Jesus Christ has become the pivotal point of the single-minded devotion of God. God has provided for himself a lamb. God has provided for himself a mediator between God and man. God has provided away for all mankind to be saved and come to know the truth. All the resources of heaven are directly related to the person and work of the Lord Jesus Christ. This is why God issues the command from heaven "hear ye him." All that has come before him are no longer relevant in the scope of God's purpose for a new thing has been instituted in the Son. That which was foretold has now come to fruition; God has made know his salvation wherein all men can be saved. He had promised Abraham that in him all the families of the earth would be blessed and the fullness of time has come to manifest the blessing. God's single-minded devotion is and always has been to fulfill his word for it is impossible for him to lie. On the mount of transfiguration, Jesus is set apart alone as the final authority to execute the will of God for all mankind.

> God who at sundry times and in divers manners spake in time past unto the fathers by the prophets, Hath in these last days spoken unto

us by his Son, whom he hath appointed heir of all
things, by whom also he made the worlds; Who
being the brightness of his glory, and the express
image of his person, and upholding all things by
the word of his power, when he had by himself
purged our sins, sat down on the right hand of
the Majesty on high. (Heb. 1:1–3, KJV)

What a blessing God has bestowed upon us that he has committed himself to, that all men may come to see and believe. The
revelation of God was under the law in the Old Testament about
the foretelling of the coming of the Christ. The revelation of God
in the New Testament is the manifestation of grace and truth by the
Lord Jesus Christ. God's single-minded devotion is proclaimed in
making known the "good news of the gospel of Jesus Christ." For
it is in Christ that God has manifested the fullness of the Godhead
bodily. It is in Christ that the sins of the whole world are taken away.
It is in Christ that the prince of this world (the devil) is judged.
All the efforts and authority of heaven are committed to building,
promoting, and executing the will of God by making sure that Jesus
Christ has the per-eminence in all things. What is per-eminence?
Pre-eminence suggest the fact that Jesus Christ is superior to and
surpasses all others known and unknown seen and unseen. God is so
single-minded in his devotion to Christ that he has placed him.

Far above all principality, and power, and
might, and dominion, and every name that is
named, not only in this world, but also in that
which is to come: And hath put all things under
his feet, and gave him to be the head over all
things to the church, which is his body, the fullness of him that filleth all in all. (Eph. 1:21–23,
KJV)

God is well pleased with his plan of salvation and the wonderful work that he has done toward the children of men in Christ

Jesus. God has been so effectively represented by the Son and his atonement that he has sat him down at his right hand. The scriptures declare that, "He is the propitiation for our sins: and not for ours only, but also for the sins of the whole world" (1 John 2:2, KJV). This is worthy of God being satisfied and willing to show forth his single-minded devotion there unto. When Jesus upon the cross of Calvary, he uttered the words "it's finished," the whole will of God was complete in that he had paid the sin debt in full securing redemption for every nation and every tongue. His life in the flesh was a representation of complete obedience to the will of God even unto death. This divine order of God was predetermined by his counsel and foreordained before the foundation of the world for his glory. God has shown forth his single-minded devotion to be toward his will. The sovereign will of God takes precedence over all things. When Jesus taught the disciples to pray, his instructions were that they would pray that "Thy will be done on earth as it is in heaven" (Matt. 6:10b, KJV). The will of God is always executed in heaven without reservation as the scriptures suggest that it is done in heaven. However, there have been hindrances to his will being done in earth because of the failure of man through sin. The Lord Jesus Christ has forever changed the dynamic of the will of God being made whole and complete. For it is written, "Then said I, lo, I come (in the volume of the book it is written of me) to do thy will, O God" (Heb. 10:7, KJV) and also while preparing to go to the cross Jesus prayed, "O, my Father, if it were possible, let this cup pass from me: nevertheless not as I will, but as thou wilt" (Matt. 26:39, KJV). The divine will of God must and will always supersede the will of man.

Surveying the single-minded devotion of God we come to understand the providence of God in relationship to the will of God. God is always at work even as the husbandman to watch over and nurture the appropriate actions that would align with his will. In the beginning, God spoke of the seed of the woman bruising the head of the serpent, a prophetic utterance about the coming of Christ. Although it wasn't until the fullness of time that God brought forth his Son who he had prepared a body, for it was told to Abraham that in him all the families of the earth would be blessed, but he and his wife would not have a child until they were both pass the age, leaving God alone as the only way to provide a child. God tells Moses to go and deliver the children of Israel out of bondage only to lead them to the impassable Red Sea, making them depend on the providence of God. Paul presents the relation between the two when he wrote:

> Wherein he hath abounded toward us in all wisdom and prudence; Having made known unto us the mystery of his will, according to his good pleasure which he hath purposed in himself: That in the dispensation of the fullness of times he might gather together; in one all things in Christ, both which are in heaven, and which are on earth even in him: In whom also we have obtained an inheritance, being predestined according to the purpose of him who worketh all things after the counsel of his own will. (Eph. 1:8–11, KJV)

Seeing that which God purposed was to be fulfilled in Christ, it behooves us to take a good look at what God has done in Christ that warrants his single-minded devotion. Paul speaks of God's purpose of gathering all things together in heaven and on earth and doing so in Christ. Let us examine this truth that we might validate God's single-minded devotion. The decree of God was set forth to provide Christ as the redeemer not only of man but also of all creation, for the whole creation is said to be groaning. "For we know that the whole creation groaneth and travail in pain until now" (Rom. 8:22, KJV). From God's perspective, heaven and earth was affected by sin, and God's purpose was to make reconciliation with man and reestablish his union with heaven and earth through Christ. All the prophecies and promises of God are based upon a New Covenant that God has established in Christ. There is a missing bond between heaven and earth that has been reunited in Christ. It is very unfortunate that we are not conscious of this missing link; however, God is and has chosen to use Christ as his answer.

The single-minded devotion of God is made known in the fact that God is not willing that any should perish but that all men be saved. God is continually dispersing his grace and mercy to the uttermost that all will be without excuse. He has provided the church to go forth with the great commission to preach the good news of the gospel. To the whole world, the cry is proclaimed to every nation, every tongue to believe on the Lord Jesus Christ and thou shall be saved. He has poured out the Holy Spirit in the earth to convict men of sin, righteousness, judgment, with the responsibility to teach and comfort. The greatest action that God has executed towards man was in the death of Christ for he said, "And I, if I be lifted up from the earth, will draw all men unto me" (John 12:32, KJV). He is touched with our infirmities and has risen from the grave to live and intercede on our behalf. This self-sacrificing love is alluring and devoted to drawing us like none other. He is the lover of our soul and because of the joy set before him he is laboring to bring many unto glory. He has also given us his word, which lives and abides forever. It is his testament of loyalty and trust worthiness; it is his exceeding great and precious promises to secure all our insecurities. It is the light and life that leads us unto all truth. All of these are working together for the good to fulfill his purpose that man will set his heart right with God!

God's single-minded devotion is made known in his desire for us to come to know the truth. Jesus alone declares of himself to be the truth. He is the embodiment of truth, his character is truth, and all that he speaks is truth, he is the True and Living God. Herein is the reason why God is so single-minded in his devotion because it is written, "And ye shall know the truth, and the truth shall make you free" (John 8:32, KJV). Nothing has brought man into such great darkness, bondage, depravity, and ignorance like the dominion of sin and death. God's revelation of Jesus Christ was also to be the deciding factor for how much truth man would desire to know. To grow in grace and in the knowledge of the Lord Jesus Christ, man would come to know truth and continue to learn to know more truth. The more truth that would be revealed to those that would diligently seek him with the whole heart, the more freedom that they would experience. The Spirit of truth is available to continually guide into all truth causing all who are yielded to his authority to live in the perfect liberty that only Christ can give. God has made it possible for man to come to know the truth about God, man, the world, sin, and the devil. Truth that he was not able to discern before, truth that was more than just mere thought. The droughts about truth throughout the ages have confounded men from all walks of life. When Jesus was before Pontius Pilate, he asked the question that has perplexed men for centuries, "What is truth?" There are belief systems all over the world, to some truth is relative, to others subjective. But God has proclaimed truth to be absolute and eternal and his providence for it is sure for he said:

> I have yet many things to say unto you, but ye cannot hear them now, Howbeit when he, the Spirit of truth, is come, he will guide you into all truth: for he shall not speak of himself; but what- soever he shall hear, that shall he speak: and will shew you things to come. (John 16:12–13, KJV)

It is the will of God that man comes to know and be established in the truth. Much knowledge and understanding has caused man in his intellect to think higher of his own thoughts than that of God's. Regardless of where men may find themselves in their thoughts about what is truth. God has concluded them to be those that are. "Ever learning, and never able to come to the knowledge of the truth" (2 Tim. 3:7, KJV).

God's single-minded devotion is built upon the testimony that he has given his Son, the Lord Jesus Christ. He alone is self-suffi- cient, and having all sufficiency brings truth into the world that was full of lies and darkness. He is more than able to proclaim truth in all sincerity.

> For by him were all things created, that are in heaven, and in the earth, visible and invisible, whether they be thrones, or dominions, or prin- cipalities, or powers: all things were created by

him and for him: and he is before all things, and
by him all things consist. (Col. 1:16–17, KJV)

No one else could even dare to speak anything close to such profound knowledge of truth. There is no one that can compare to reason about or even mention in the same conversation with any equality. Many may question the integrity, authenticity, and even the reality of the person and work of the Lord Jesus Christ. But the truth of the matter is that all the questions can never negate the historical truth, the biblical truth, the absolute truth, of the gospel truth. Therefore, in answering the question that has perplexed men for centuries, "What is truth?" Jesus said, "Thy word is truth" (John 17:17b, KJV). In searching the scriptures, we see clearly the heart of God and his thoughts about his word. He has magnified his word above his name (Ps.138:2, KJV), heaven and earth shall pass away but my words shall not pass away (Matt. 24:35, KJV), the word of God is living and powerful (Heb. 4:12a, KJV), the words that I speak unto you are spirit and life (John 6:63b, KJV), "Thy word is a lamp unto my feet, and a light unto my path" (Ps. 119:105, KJV), "Faith cometh by hearing, and hearing by the word of God" (Rom. 10:17, KJV), "Man shall not live by bread alone, but by every word that proceeded out of the mouth of God" (Matt. 4:4, KJV). These thoughts and proclamations of the word of God are written for our learning and admonition that we might have hope in the scriptures.

8

God's Humbling of Himself

Who is like unto the LORD our God, who
dwelleth on high, who humbleth
himself to behold the things that are
in heaven, and in the earth!

—Psalms 113:5–6 (KJV)

The awe and wonder that is associated with the fact that the God of the universe would even consider humbling himself to draw near unto his creation, is worthy of all adoration and praise! David writes this psalm with a view of the Most High God that very few of us come to recognize. He is so awe struck and overwhelmed that his heart is excited with unspeakable joy that causes him to cry out, "Who is like unto the LORD our God! What a revelation of the tenderness and loving-kindness of Almighty God. It is almost incomprehensible to think that God would think on his creation in such a fashion as this. This is not just a casual occurrence that God would give himself to partake in; this was motivated by his innermost thoughts and regards toward his creation. It adds to David's earlier reflection upon God when he asked the question, "What is man that thou art mindful of him? And the son of man that thou visitest him?" He is convinced that such a great honor that God has put on man warrants attention and an appropriate response. What an impression that God was making upon David! What was God trying to convey about himself that he wanted all men to see? As we approach this idea, let us attempt to enter into the passion that David here exemplifies as he considers the Majesty on high. "O the depth of the riches both of the wisdom and knowledge of God! How unsearchable are his judgments, and his ways past finding out!" (Rom. 11:33, KJV). We see the greatness of God in his grandeur and glory in this expression of him humbling himself. Let us continue to examine this precious moment to witness that which David discovered.

In order to grasp the sheer magnitude of this glorious work of God, we must identify with where he dwells. David declares that he dwelleth on high. If we could only imagine that the transcendence of the Omnipresence of God, whose realm of occupancy is above the heavens, and whose foot stool is said to be the earth, it would be mind-bottling. Yet this unfathomable action of God is even more than that. Can you conceive the idea of God stepping out of eternity to look into time and space for a moment just because he is God? God forbid! The thoughts and actions of an Omniscient God cannot be categorized as vain and without substance. He does things with intentions and foreknowledge even based upon the counsel of his own will. So it gives good reason for David to express great expectancy and joy as he acknowledges the greatness of God beholding his creation. "O LORD our Lord, how excellent is thy name in all the earth! Who has set thy glory above the heavens?" (Ps. 8:1, KJV). Nothing less than a holy wonder and awe is to be exhibited at the thought of where God dwells in relationship to how he takes intimate notice of man. David observes these things with the utmost admiration for his Excellency manifested in this divine condescension towards man. God dwells in the highest heavens and in that realm man is ignorant at best of its activity. However, we do get a glimpse through the eyes of the apostle Paul.

He wrote:

> I knew a man in Christ above fourteen
> years ago, (whether in the body, I cannot tell;
> or whether out of the body, I cannot tell: God

knoweth;) such a one caught up to the third heaven. And I knew such a man, (whether in the body, or out of the body, I cannot tell God knoweth;) How that he was caught up into paradise, and heard unspeakable words, which it is not lawful for a man to utter. (2 Cor. 12:2–4, KJV)

The third heaven is the dwelling place of God and angels and the place where we know little to nothing about. In this reference, Paul gives us a peek at a few things worthy of our discussion about where God dwells. There is a distinction that is dually noted between the heavens, the sky that is within our view is considered the first heaven. The glorious display of the stars and all the glory of the galaxies is the second heaven. Then there is the third heaven that which eye hath not seen nor can see as we gaze upwards. Paul speaks of this as the high heavens, the heaven of heavens wherein God dwells. It is only by revelation that he is caught up to view this habitation of celestial glory. The one thing that he is sure of is that God dwells there; he was not even sure that he was still in his natural body. It was also there in the third heaven that he identifies being also caught up into paradise. In the midst of this divine revelation, Paul conveys to us that he has heard things that are unlawful to repeat in the earthly realm.

In the book of the Revelation, the apostle John ascribes his experience of heaven as where God's throne is. He gives us a little more insight as he recognizes God in his glory being praised and worshipped without ceasing. He writes, "And they rest not day and night, saying; Holy, holy, holy Lord God Almighty, which was, and is, and is to come" (Rev. 4:8b, KJV). In heaven, God is seen in the beauty of his holiness and given the praise, glory, and honor that he alone is worthy of. With that being said, we can surely understand the significance of God humbling himself to behold his creation. In the fullness of time when Christ was born of a virgin, he left his glory in heaven to partake of humanity. We only know in part about the intricate details of God becoming a man. But the scriptures do reveal a beautiful display of the humbling of God. Christ Jesus, who being in the form of God, thought it not robbery to be equal with God; but made himself of no reputation and took upon him the form of a servant and was made in the likeness of men. And being found in fashion as a man, he humbled himself, and became obedient unto death, even the death of the cross (Phil. 2:6–8, KJV). The very act of God leaving his glory in heaven to partake of humanity, for the purpose of identifying with sin and death that he might destroy it is, awe-inspiring. Therefore David proclaims, "Who is like unto the LORD our God! Who is like you among the god's, O LORD? Who is like you majestic in holiness? Awesome in praises, working wonders? (Exod. 15:11, KJV). For who in the heaven can be compared unto the LORD? Who among the sons of the mighty can be likened unto the Lord? (Ps. 89:6, KJV). No matter how far we search, or to what extent we may imagine, we will still come to the same conclusion to this question. "Forasmuch as there is none like unto thee, O LORD; thou art great, and thy name is great in might" (Jer. 10:6, KJV). There is none that can compare to the Only True and Living God!

What does God say of himself concerning these things that he has chosen to behold.

> For thus saith the high and lofty One that inhabiteth eternity, whose name is Holy; I dwell in the high and holy place, with him also that is of a contrite and humble spirit, to revive the spirit of the humble, and to revive the heart of the contrite ones. For I will not contend for ever, neither will I be always wroth: for the spirit should fail before me, and the souls which I have made. (Isa. 57:15–16, KJV)

God's humbling of himself was a divine testimony of humiliation. Taking a deeper inside look at the work involved with God humbling himself we will be amazed at the innermost thoughts of God. It was a necessity for God to take on the nature of man to fulfill his purpose and in doing so he was clothing himself with humiliation. The predetermined sufferings of Christ testify to the truth of God humbling himself and adorning himself with such humiliation through his sufferings. The truth that God was manifested in the flesh was manifested in Christ destined to suffer for our good and his glory. For it became him, for who are all things, in bringing many sons unto glory, to make the captain of their salvation perfect through suffering (Heb. 2:10, KJV). The glory of God is intimately connected to the suffering and humiliation of Christ and this concept passes our understanding. Some of the forethoughts about the sufferings of Christ are less than to be desired. It is no coincidence that the things that God proposed in bringing forth Christ to suffer for our sins is truly hard to believe. It is even recorded that the prophet Isaiah asked the question, "Who hath believed our report?" The things that he proclaimed about the sufferings of Christ would cause many to question the rationale behind it. He stated of Christ that:

> He hath neither form nor comeliness; and when we shall see him; there is no beauty that we should desire him. He is despised and rejected of men; a man of sorrows, acquainted with grief: and we hid as it were our faces from him; he was despised, and we esteemed him not. Surely he hath home our griefs, and carried our sorrows: and yet we did esteem him stricken, smitten of God, and afflicted. But he was wounded for our transgressions, he was bruised for our iniquities; the chastisement of our peace was upon him; and with his stripes we are healed. (Isa. 53:2b–5, KJV)

Oh, how wonderful! Oh, how marvelous! Is our Savior's love for us? No one took his life according to the scriptures; he laid it down on his own accord. He despised the shame and suffering that he endured by being made sin to pay our sin debt. But he looked pass all of the pain, shame, humiliation, and suffering with his sights only on the joy of having you in relationship with him for all eternity. It is impossible to enter into his joy or even grasp it without understanding the reality of him being jealous for his creation and the work of his hands. Yes, he was oppressed, abused, judged, and imprisoned yet without complaint or even opening his mouth. He was whipped, beyond recognition, spit on, crucified, and buried just to get back that which rightly belonged to him. For it is he who hath created us and not we ourselves. Creation was God's idea, creating man in his image was his will and being pleased enough with his work to conclude that it was "very good" was his thoughts. The words *very good* coming from me or you does not carry the value and validity of their sound coming across our lips. But those words coming out of the mouth of the Only Wise God, the Only True and Living God, him alone who has all power in heaven and earth, means more than we give merit to. This was the only way to please God's holy and righteous judgment and make Christ the complete satisfaction for the penalty of sin and death.

This is the reason why it was so significant that Christ humbled himself and became obedient unto death. By taking on the form of a servant and obeying the dictates of the sovereign will of God in shame and humiliation, he was manifesting the wisdom and power of God. There is nothing too hard for God. It was not hard for God to create another way to bring glory to his name in his creation. It was not hard for him to destroy the works of the devil. It was not hard for God to secure all the insecurities and fears of man. It was not hard for God to deal with all the past, present, and future sins of all mankind. The redeeming work of the cross of Christ brought life into a dead world. It brought hope to those who all their lifetime was without hope. It brought together man and God who by the nature of sin and holiness opposed and each other.

> That at that time ye were without Christ,
> being aliens from the commonwealth of Israel,
> and strangers from the covenants of promise,
> having no hope, and without God in the world;
> but now in Christ Jesus ye who sometimes were

far off are made nigh by the blood of Christ. For he is our peace, who hath made both one, and hath broken down the middle wall of partition between us; Having abolished in his flesh the enmity, even the law of commandments contained in ordinances; for to make in himself of twain one new man, so making peace; And that he might reconcile both unto God in one body by the cross, having slain the enmity thereby. (Eph. 2:12–16, KJV)

Yes, Jesus did it all and all to him we owe. For God summed all things up in Christ.

Be not dismayed by this tragedy of brutal humiliation, for it also made him alone worthy of exaltation. Now that God's judgment has been satisfied, because it is impossible for him to lie, death had to be accomplished. Christ tasted death for every man born of the flesh as a substitutionary representation for the glory of God. Hallelujah! He was given the power over death. God did not stop at satisfying his judgment. He did a new thing, first by raising Christ from the dead. He now has made man free from the judgment of sin and death; he chose to create a new man in Christ. The humbling of God put to death all the enemies of God and man in the flesh and spirit. It is the fantastic work of death that by the amazing grace of God would bring life to man through the resurrection of the dead. If we are to appreciate the fact that God humbled himself to behold the things that are in heaven and earth. If we are to recognize that Christ thought that it was not robbery to be equal with God but humbled himself and became obedient unto the death of the cross. It would behoove us to accept the reality that the incurable disease of sin that has devastated man and warrants all the displeasure of God provoked him unto jealousy for his creation. The most devastating aspect of the nature of sin is that it made man disobedient by nature to the Most High God. Disobedience is such a contradiction to the character of God as it defies his laws and commandments, it resist his person and warrants his wrath. But God who is rich in mercy look passed man's fault and saw his need.

God saw that man needed a Savior, he saw that there was none that could help, and he looked down through eternity and saw that he had to save man for himself, from himself, by himself.

> According as he hath chosen us in him before the foundation of the world, that we should be holy and without blame before him in love: Having predestination us unto adoption of children by Jesus Christ himself, according to the good pleasure of his will. (Eph. 1:4–5, KJV)

We find yourself revisiting the will of God as he purposed within himself. What God has determined to be of and for his good pleasure will not be disallowed. He will accomplish that which he purposed according to his will. God knew what it would take to work out the redemptive plans that he designed. He also was intentional in preparing the way to execute his plans. Jesus Christ was a lamb slain before the foundation of the world to take away the sin of the world. God humbled himself in considering what and how he would bring this great salvation to man. Who is like unto Our God! He is touched with our infirmities and has given Christ to be our mediator between God and man. He has forever been ordained as our high priest to ever live and make intercession on our behalf.

> Wherefore he is able also to save them to the uttermost that comes to God by him, seeing he ever liveth to make intercession for them. For such an high priest became us, who is holy, harmless, undefiled, separate from sinners, and made higher than the heavens: who needeth not daily, as those high priest, to offer up sacrifice, first for his own sins, and then for the people's for this he did once, when he offered up himself. (Heb. 8:25–27, KJV)

Let us conclude with the divine appointment of Christ to die once and for all as marvelous in our eyes. Let it provoke in us the awe and wonder that David experienced when he viewed this glorious picture of God, humbling himself to behold what was in heaven and earth. May we like him shout the praise of knowing that there is no God like our God!

9

God's Exclusive Right

Look unto me, and be saved, all
the ends of the earth:
for I am God, and there is none else.

—Isaiah 45:22 (KJV)

When we first open the pages of scripture, we learn immediately the most important truth that they possess. God created, God said, God saw, God divided, God set, God made, God formed, God caused, God took, and God blessed. The book of Genesis opens its dialogue declaring without reservation God! There is much to be said about God alone that if all of the books ever written were about him, they would cover the whole earth and not tell it all. However, the Bible has revealed throughout its pages that God has an exclusive right to his claims and creation. The thoughts and judgments of God are decisive and without question as he declares who he is and the immutability of his counsel. God's exclusive right is based upon the absolute truth that he declares about himself, "I am God, and there is none else." There is no one, or nothing, that has an inherit right, to loyalty or allegiance like God. But man has over the history of humanity proven to make choices contrary that would make him servant to obey anything. As we continue to build upon the idea that God is jealous for you, we must survey God's exclusive right. What do we mean when we say God's exclusive right? In terms of a legal expression, exclusive right maintains the thought that God has the prerogative and power of one who is sovereign to all claims to perform or prohibit. He has a monopoly on the claims that he is God alone. He is dominant in creation in that no one else has created anything. In the beginning was the Word, and the Word was with God, and the Word was God. The same was in the beginning with God. All things were made by him; and without him was not anything made that was made (John 1:13, KJV). Along with the fact that God has exclusive right as the True and Living God, he also possesses Sole right as Creator and Originator seeing that no one could ever reproduce that which he has created. David wrote:

> Bless the LORD, O my soul. O LORD my God, thou art very great thou art clothed with honor and majesty. Who coverst thyself with light as with a garment: who stretches out the heavens like a curtain: who layeth the beams of his chambers in the waters: who walketh upon the wings of the wind. (Ps. 104: 1–3, KJV)

The narrative of creation speaks of how great and greatly to be praised God is for the display of his power. This description of his greatness reveals his authority over light, the winds, and waters. Such greatness has never been seen or heard of in any other, but the invisible God claims them as he expresses his inherent attributes. The Divine Artist at work in creation developed an eternal masterpiece that is full of awe and wonder. The things that are seen were not made of things which appear (the sky was not made from the sky, and neither was the stars made from stars or the mountains of their own). Even the voice of the sun is heard throughout the universe but not of its own accord. God has the inherent, exclusive right alone, to proclaim on his own authority that he is who, and how, he says he is.

In our scripture verse for examination, God states to all, "Look unto me." He does not instruct us to look unto man, history, ideology, philosophy, religion, science or knowledge, but unto himself period. What is he requiring of us in this simple yet provocative directive? The call and requirement of God has been the same to all and upon all—the call to obey. God spoke through Moses:

> Now therefore, if ye will obey my voice indeed, and keep my covenant then ye shall be a peculiar treasure unto me above all people: for the earth is mine." (Exod. 19:5, KJV)
>
> That thou mayest love the LORD thy God, and that thou mayest obey his voice, and that thou mayest cleave unto him: for he is thy life, and the length of thy days. (Deut. 30:2oa, KJV)
>
> But this thing commanded I them saying, Obey my voice, and I will be your God, and ye shall be my people. (Jer. 9:23a, KJV)

God has always and will always require that we obey his voice. God speaking from his exclusive right to direct and instruct in the way that we should go will always parallel his purpose and will. We will speak further on this subject in more detail in the preceding chapter; however, the operative word for our admonition is "obey." We will never enter into a better understanding of the whole counsel and complete will of God without a willing mind to obey. Because God is Omnipotent, Omnipresence, and Omniscience, he is more than able to order our steps aright.

Upon our willingness to obey his voice, we become the beneficiary of his reward; in this particular exhortation, it is to be saved. Look unto me and be saved! Understanding the implications of God being jealous for you will have clear insight to his aim and protection for your good. As I stated in my opening paragraph, man has a tendency to obey anything and thus leading him into all sorts of darkness and bondage. As God exerts and imposes his exclusive right as God, he is opposed to us all having anything or anyone ruling in our life as god other than him. He knows that there is no other God, but he also knows that none other has the same single-minded devotion as he does when it comes to the care of his creatures. Jesus said, "Behold the fowls of the air: for they sow not, neither do they reap, nor gather into barns, yet your heavenly Father feedeth them. Are ye not much better than they" (Matt. 6:26, KJV)? Salvation is of the LORD. It has never been thee though of man that he needs to be saved. We may have salvation upon our hearts and minds when facing immediate fears and dangers. But God looks upon the whole man and not just the circumstances that he is experiencing. We need to be saved from our ignorance of God, we need to be saved from yourself, we need to be saved from the work of the devil and ultimately we need to be saved from sin and the wrath of God. God knows our state and he is acquainted with all of our thoughts before we are. Therefore, we must see the need to recognize God's ultimate right over his creation as he has our best interest in mind. What does God mean by look unto me and be saved?

The thought of looking unto God implies, first looking away from all others and distractions that do hinder us from looking unto him. Looking unto him carries the idea of focusing our will, intellect, and emotions on who he is and the very fact that "He is." Seeing that no man has seen God at any time and the fact that God is a spirit and indeed invisible, faith is an absolute necessity. But without faith, it is impossible to please him: for him that cometh to God must believe that he is, and that he is a rewarder of them who diligently seek him (Heb. 11:4, KJV). God has the exclusive right not only to challenge us to look unto him, but also he has the exclusive right to instruct us how to do it. He has chosen the means of faith. It is interesting to see how detail orientated God is in instructing us to look unto him. He tells us we are to seek him diligently with the whole heart. He cannot and will not be approached haphazardly for it will infringe upon the fact that he is Holy and worthy of our utmost respect. No man can just approach the unapproachable God, but he has provided the means and the way wherein he can be approached if we would but obey. To look unto the LORD means that we position yourself to trust him and all of his judgments. It means that we do not depend on our thoughts but acknowledge our dependency on him alone. To look unto the Lord means that we surrender to him giving him the exclusive right to work in us both the will and the actual doing of his good pleasure. Because God has the exclusive right to his creation, it is also one of the determining factors and cause for his jealousy.

In the continuing thought of the scripture that we are examining, God said, "All the ends of the earth." No one is exempt from his exclusive right and call to all mankind, every nation, every tongue, every culture, everywhere upon the face of the entire earth. This literally means that the absolute exclusive right that God has over all is upon all that they may come to a place to obey him. That all men may come to a place to look unto the LORD and be saved. God, in his forbearance of man, has shown his willingness to make his providence available that man would be without excuse. It is his will that man would be dependent upon him alone and no other. God gave man a free will to choose, but it has been the will of God for man to choose to obey the LORD, and he has not.

> Seek ye the LORD while he may be found, call upon him while he is near: Let the wicked forsake his way, and the unrighteous man his thoughts: and let him return unto the LORD, and he will abundantly pardon. For my thoughts are not your thoughts, neither are your ways my ways, saith the LORD. (Isa. 55:6–8, KJV)

Those that will obey and look unto the LORD will be saved for he has made provisions for man to be abundantly pardoned. Therefore, whosoever will let him seek, from the ends of the earth let him call upon the LORD. God in his jealousy contends against all other claims to be god, and he resists the proud giving grace unto the humble. But it is his exclusive right as the Only True and Living God to make himself known as he is and proclaim his salvation to the ends of the earth.

He gives his reason, "For I am God, and there is none else." God separates himself from any and all potential candidates that would become idols. He knows that he is God alone and that there is none else; therefore, he exposes the lie that has distorted the minds of many. There are those from generation to generation that have claims of worship of another God, who is no God. One nation to the next fills their heart and imagination with their claims of another God. However controversial that it may be in the mind and lives of all who would think that there is another God, there is none. This is the result of man becoming vain in his imagination, as well as the result of being deceived by Satan himself.

> For God to declare that he is God and there is none else he is including every other thought about a God that ever existed in the earth. I am the Lord, and there is none else, there is no God beside me: I girded thee, though thou hast not known me: that they may know from the rising of the sun, and from the west, that there is none beside me, I am the Lord and there is none else. (Isa. 45:5–6, KJV)

No other being can promote the claims of being omnipotent, omniscient, and omnipresent. There is no one else that is eternal, self-existent, and self-sufficient. If he is God alone, then all others are liars because he has proven them to be so by the testimony of his works. God has the exclusive right to claim his power and authority over all the earth as the only true God. This is one of the major causes that provokes God unto jealousy as he witness the ignorance of man giving glory and honor to something or someone that has claimed to be God. The falsehood associated with this these claims has led many into captivity over the history of humanity, yet God remains true.

God must be true to himself, to the scriptures, and to the Church.

> Having made known to us the mystery of his will, according to his good pleasure which he hath purposed in himself. That in the dispensation of time he might gather together in one all things in Christ, both which are in heaven and which are on earth; even in him. (Eph. 1:9–10, KJV)

What God has done throughout biblical history and what he has purposed to do throughout eternity has all been defined in Christ. He has made himself known as the Only Wise God. What God has done in Christ is in fact a testimony of his exclusive right as God. Jesus Christ was given the responsibility to make God known to the world; he was the express image of the person of God. Everything that he did was a direct act of obedience to the sovereign will of God. Everything that was fulfilled by him in scripture was design by God for the glory of God. God being true to himself he is a God of light and in him is no darkness at all. It is his responsibility to make known the truth about himself and present it in such a fashion that is consistent with his person. Again, it was necessary for God to determine what would be the most effective way to make him known and execute his righteous judgment, while giving man hope in this world. By his exclusive right as God, he chose to do all things through Christ. It also is a testament to the greatness of his power as God and the work of his hands as he validates by what he has purposed within himself.

Thou art God alone! Is the proclamation as he has proven with many infallible proofs, and there is no one else. What is man that he thinks that his thoughts and assessments about God warrant any credible validation. Too often, man has thought higher of his own thoughts than he should and devalued the thoughts of God as if their judgment is just and true. The God of the Bible has set forth in the scriptures what is just and true because he is God alone and it is impossible for him to lie.

> For who hath known the mind of the LORD? Or who hath been his counselor? Or who hath first given to him, and it shall be recompensed unto him again? For of him, and through him and to him, are all things: to whom he glory forever. Amen. (Rom. 11:34–36, KJV)

God's exclusive right to boldly proclaim the truth about himself is his alone. No man hath seen God at any time, and no one can speak expressively about him better than himself. God has the exclusive right to be God, speak as God and execute his righteous judgments as God. It is true that we have a variety of belief systems all over the earth, in every nation and every tongue. But it is interesting to note that God has said, "Every way of a man is right in his own eyes: but the LORD pondereth the hearts" (Prov. 21:2, KJV). Man has been so vulnerable especially when it comes to matters pertaining to God. It has been proven over the years that man has chosen to believe some of anything about God in his ignorance.

> Because that, when they knew God, they
> glorified him not as God, neither was thankful:
> But became vain in their imaginations, and their
> foolish heart was darkened. Professing themselves
> to be wise, they became fools and changed the
> glory of the uncorruptible God into image made
> like corruptible man and birds, and four footed
> beast and creeping things. (Rom. 1:21–23, KJV)

Our view of God is of the utmost importance because it will determine how we respond to him as well as how we live before him. That being said, it is even more important to God seeing that he desires man to know him in the truth. God has made known that he is a jealous God and it is also within his exclusive right to be such. He has reserved the right to reveal the knowledge of his person only to those that seek him with the whole heart diligently. God has placed a high value on knowing the True and Living God because such knowledge is wonderful. It is high, and we cannot just attain to it. Unfortunately, we live in a day and age where knowing God is not a priority, knowing God seems to be superficial or an option that we can live without. God gave man a free will to choose; however, he also charges us to choose him.

> I call heaven and earth to record this day
> against you that I have set before your life and
> death, blessing and cursing: therefore choose life
> that both thou and thy seed may live: That thou

mayest love the LORD thy God, and that thou mayest obey his voice, and cleave unto him: for he is thy life, and the length of thy days. (Deut. 30:19–20a, KJV)

In light of the wonderful works of God that he has done toward the children of men, he has the exclusive right to do whatsoever he pleases.

10

God's Vehement Desire

Hath the LORD *as great delight in*
burnt offerings and sacrifices,
as in obeying the voice of the LORD*?*
Behold, to obey is better than
sacrifice, and hearken than the fat of rams.

—1 Samuel 15:22

Learning to know God brings such unspeakable joy that it is hard to try and convey the thing that he is so passionate about because it brings so much sadness. It brings such sadness because man is prone to do the very thing that God does not desire and that is disobedience. The zeal of the LORD is consumed with his strong passion for obedience. It should not be a hard thing to conceive that the Creator of heaven and earth and all that therein is not only has an exclusive right toward the obedience desired, but he is worthy of it. Imagine for a moment God creating the heavens, the earth, the sea, fowls of the air and beast of the fields. Then he decides to create man in his image to be his representation in the earth with dominion over his creation and all that he desires for him is good and he decides to disobey. His act of disobedience would set creation on course for hell and destruction as everyone thereafter born of the flesh would inherit the same spirit of disobedience. No one born of the flesh will ever really appreciate the damning truth of the offensive nature of disobedience to the only True, Living, Holy God. Disobedience is such a devastating act of rebellion against God that it defies his person and, disrespects his authority. "For rebellion is as the sin of witchcraft, and stubbornness is as iniquity and idolatry" (1 Sam. 15:23a, KJV). The stubborn rebellion that is rooted in the heart of man so disdains that God equates it to witchcraft and idolatry. It is against the backdrop of this imagery that we will look at God's vehement desire.

Any association with witchcraft is a gross undertaking of darkness and fellowship with devils. Such activity is full of dangers as it positions one to be an abomination to God. What is an abomination? It is such evil that it causes detestation, disgrace, and disgust. Disobedience is an atrocity to the claims of the Most High God of being God! God does not take lightly this offense to his authority and sovereignty accountable, and that he doesn't exist. The disobedience that has plagued mankind has easily categorized him as being fools because of the darkness of their hearts. This act of rebellion against God needs to be understood from its inherent residual damage. What are we guilty of rebelling against? We are guilty of rebelling against the authority of the word of God. Resisting God's control and exclusive right to instruct us in the way that we should go. Rebellion is in fact an act of violence against the sovereign rule of the Almighty God! Oh to be able to understand the depth of this infringement upon the person and character of God.

The pride of man has deceived him into thinking less about God and more about himself to the extent that he has become stubborn. Man is so obstinate that he is determined not to change his attitude toward God on his own accord even if valid arguments suggest that it's to his benefit. Generation after generation within every nation upon the face of the earth, every race, and every culture that which is flesh is flesh, and everyone is guilty. Herein is the reason that God is so adamant about his demand for obedience. The spirit of disobedience has prevented God from being who he is in his creation that he created in his image, man. "For as by one man's disobedience many were made sinners so also by one Man's obedience many will be made righteous" (Rom. 5:19, KJV). God's vehement desire is obedience, for it alone can bring the glory and honor designed by him in man. Obeying the voice of the LORD is the fuel that lights the fire of the delight of God. Obedience is that sweet smelling aroma that arises into the nostril of God that satisfies his appetite of pleasure like none other. God was the initiator in teaching the children of Israel to worship him as he instructed them through Moses. There are many things that we can learn about the Most High God through the examples that he has given us in this vital history. We will now focus our attention on some of the lessons that God was teaching us through his interaction with the children of Israel. Again, it is imperative that we understand that they did not know God. Moses did not know God, God was the initiator and bringing to them this excellent knowledge.

When God first called Moses, he drew Moses unto himself by appearing to him in a flame of fire in the midst of a bush. Moses was not seeking after God he was keeping the flock of his father in law minding his own business. This information is vital to our understanding because it also validates the truth that God chooses us we don't choose him, God seeks us we do not seek him. And Moses said:

> I will now turn aside, and see this great
> sight, why the bush is not burnt. And when the
> LORD saw that he turned aside to see, God called
> unto him out of the midst of the bush, and said
> Moses, Moses. And he said, Here am I. (Exod.
> 3:3–4, KJV)

Likewise, Noah was not seeking God the scriptures inform us that he found grace in the eyes of the LORD, and Abraham was visited and called to obey God's instructions without even knowing who God was. These instances will become more valuable to us as we learn to see and understand the works of God's hand. I would like for you to look with me at the priceless truths that God has made known about his vehement desire for obedience through the eyes of Moses. As God used Moses to lead the children of Israel out of Egypt toward the will of God for their lives, it was obedience that God continually conveyed as his aim. The most beautiful and detailed insight that we gather about God's vehement desire for obedience is from God revelation of law and his instructions for the tabernacle. We all may be familiar with the Ten Commandments, as a direct imperative from God for obedience, but it also reveals that God demands obedience. He does not ask man to obey, he commands that man obey. I might add here that when God created Adam and placed him in the garden, there was only one command from God, and that was "of the tree of the knowledge of good and evil thou shalt not eat." God being true to his Holy nature still demanded obedience.

We cannot rationalize in our minds why God demands our obedience as if we have some sense of better judgment than him. If we take heed to ourselves and the thoughts that God has made known about himself, we shall forever reap the benefits of the truth making us free. Let us continue to examine this idea about obedience being God's vehement desire. The Ten Commandments served more than one purpose; yes, they were designed to challenge us to obey God. They were also used to prove our love for God and others. Even more important as they revealed our utter failure to be obedient they would create within us a conscious need for Christ. The Ten Commandments made us know that nothing should prevent our obedience to God. They caused us to look at God's view of how relationship to him should be. They provoked us to not be flippant in our thoughts about God but have a healthy fear of the LORD. They also demanded of us separation, consecration, and sanctification as God's children. They taught the need for fundamental respect for authority within the family structure, relationships and even human life. The Ten Commandments would develop honesty, integrity, truthfulness that nurtured peace and contentment. These things were all for our good and God's glory that made obedience more than a necessity. God commanded obedience because man did not choose to obey. God commanded obedience because he knew that man would see his inability to satisfy its demand and be found guilty.

When we take a closer look at God bringing to man his thoughts about worship, the first thing that we see is obedience. When Moses was before the LORD for forty days and forty nights, God gave him

specific instructions in regards to building a tabernacle for the purpose of worship. The first act of obedience required of God was that
everyone would willingly bring an offering to build the tabernacle.
What really are very intriguing about the whole orchestration of the
tabernacle is the implicit details to strict obedience. Their obedience
had to be willingly, the materials had to be specific colors, specific
textures, and specific scents. There were given specific measurements,
specific designs, specific shapes, designations, specific workers, and
specific tribe of people even to exercise the priesthood. There was
specific order, specific animals, portions, and specific instructions for
every aspect of preparation to worship. And let them make me a
sanctuary; that I may dwell among them. "According to all that I
shew thee. After the pattern of the Tabernacle, and the pattern of
all the instruments thereof, even so shall ye make it" (Exod. 25:8–9,
KJV). God has by design created the atmosphere for obedience to
be complied with that in all things man may learn how to approach
God, live before God, worship God, and serve God. Everything he
required was to be done according to all that he said do. God never
suggested or gave man the liberty to implement any of his thoughts
pertaining to the things of God.

God demands obedience in all things that he might make his
presence known and manifest his glory. In all the things that the
commandments and the law required and all that the sacrifices and
offerings would temporarily provide, Christ fulfilled.

> Knowing that a man is not justified by the
> works of the law, but by the faith of Jesus Christ,
> that we might be justified by the faith of Christ,
> and not by the works of the law: for by the works
> of the law shall no flesh be justified. (Gal. 2:16,
> KJV)

Obedience that God desired was made complete when Jesus
came in the flesh and became obedient even unto the death of the
cross. All of the demands of the law and commandments were completely satisfied; all the sacrifices and offerings were elevated in the

onetime offering of Christ himself. And that he died for all, that they which live should not henceforth live unto themselves, but unto him which died for them and rose again.

> Wherefore henceforth know we no man after the flesh: yea, though we have known Christ after the flesh, yet now henceforth know us him no more. Therefore if any man be in Christ, he is a new creature: old things are passed away; behold all things are become new. (2 Cor. 5:15–17, KJV)

God's vehement desired for obedience is now finished for what was impossible for man to do in the flesh God sent his only begotten Son to accomplish. Now he has committed all things to the Son and the requirements to please God has changed for he has been pleased in the Son.

God's vehement desire now is not just for obedience but for obedience to the faith. Paul wrote concerning this faith in Jesus Christ that he was "declared to be the Son of God with power, according to the spirit of holiness, by the resurrection from the dead: By whom we have received grace and apostleship, for obedience to the faith among all nations, for his name" (Rom. 1:4–5, KJV). Behold, all things are new and under a new covenant, which has been sealed and written in the blood of Christ. God is so vehement about obedience that he demands perfection. Perfection is consistent with his nature and character. We look at perfection as something unattainable and beyond our capability, but God sees it as normal and mandatory. God desires that we serve him with a perfect heart; he desires that we behave in a perfect way; he will keep us in perfect peace. He will perfect that which concerns us, make our faith perfect, establish us in perfect love, present us perfect in Christ. "Be ye therefore perfect, even as your Father which is in heaven is perfect" (Matt. 5:48, KJV). Obeying the voice of the LORD is and will always be our victory. Now that everything has been committed to the Son, God has called upon us to look unto Jesus the author and finisher of our faith. We are to look away from the thoughts and judgments and witnesses of the Old Testament for defining how we view God. We are to take the scriptures that were written for our admonition, but all its claims have been summed up in Christ. He has become our all in all for the glory of God and the fulfilling of his purpose that has been ordained before the foundation of the world. God's vehement desire is now that we surrender to Jesus Christ as our Lord and Savior and hear and obey his voice.

Jesus said:

> For I came down from heaven, not to do mine own will, but the will of him that sent me. And this is the Father's will which hath sent me, that of all which he hath given me I should lose nothing, but should raise it up again the last day. And this is the will of him that sent me, that everyone which seeth the Son and believeth on him, may have everlasting life: and I will raise him up the last day. (John 6:38–40, KJV)

God has spoken and is yet speaking through his Son Jesus Christ for he is the expressed image of his person. He has all power in heaven and earth and God has committed all judgment to the Son. Jesus Christ as the author and finisher of faith exhorts all that would come unto him to believe on him unto everlasting life. The call of the Lord Jesus is a call to obey his instructions to submit to the will of God, submit to the righteousness of God, and submit to the judgment of God. The instructions are to be obedient to the faith of the gospel. Believe that Jesus Christ died for you and your sinfulness to deliver you from sin and death. Believe that God raised him from the dead to justify you forever with the forgiveness of sins. Believe that God s righteousness is in Christ Jesus and his righteousness is given to you once you believe in him. Believe that all have sinned and fall short of the glory of God. God's vehement desire is that all men believe the testimony that he has given his Son.

> He that believeth on the Son of God hath the witness in himself: he that believeth not God hath made him a liar; because he believeth not made the record that God gave of his Son. And this is the record that God hath given to us eternal life, and this life is in his Son. (1 John 5:10–11, KJV)

God's vehement desire is built upon his strong passion and ardent resolve for executing mercy, justice, judgment, and truth. To protect and maintain his honor, to exhibit his holiness and uphold righteousness. God's vehement desire is a constant and prevalent aspect of him being a jealous God as he makes his presence known as the Only True God. God's vehement desire is always in relationship to the truth of his word and his faithfulness to magnify it. God's vehement desire is for all men everywhere to repent and return unto the LORD. To exercise the godly sorrow warranted for such an offense toward a Holy God. The apostle Paul validated the benefit of such repentance toward God.

> For godly sorrow worketh repentance to salvation not to be repented of: but the sorrow of the world worketh death. For behold this self-same thing, that ye sorrowed after a godly sort, what carefulness it wrought in you, yea, what clearing of yourselves, yea what indignation, yea, what fear, yea what vehement desire, yea, what zeal, yea, what revenge! In all things ye have approved yourselves to be clear this matter. (2 Cor. 7:10–11, KJV)

Hallelujah and Amen for God's vehement desire!

11

━━━━●)((●))(●━━━━

God's Love Displayed

*For God so loved the world, that he gave his only
begotten Son, that whosoever
believeth in him should
not perish, but have everlasting life.*

—John 3:16 (KJV)

This particular scripture has been utilized so much in so many venues with good intentions, I might add. However, to some degree, I do believe the sensationalization of it has caused the significance of God's love being openly displayed, for a lost and dying world, has gotten lost. We see John 3:16 address at countless sporting events, quick shots on the television from footage of fans celebrating their favorite sports teams. We see it on billboards, cars, graffiti on walls, and yes, some have even wore it on their body. It is possible that because of it being so casually utilized with such frequency that we have become immune to the reality of it. But this act of love is more than wonderful, more than awe inspiring, more than marvelous! It is my hope, desire, and prayer as we attempt to go behind the scenes and get a glimpse at the thoughts and heart of God, that we can rekindle affection for a first love, for this greatest love ever displayed. Yes, it is good news worthy to be published and shouted out abroad, but it is also a divine truth parallel to nothing ever experienced in the history of humanity on the face of the earth. God so loved the world, has far reaching implications that cannot be easily overlooked. What is within this thought "so loved" that we can uncover that will help us get in touch with the heart of God? This small yet powerful particle carries with it eternal emphasis that magnifies God's act of love exponentially. The degree of this love is exceedingly, abundantly, above that which we could ever imagine or think. God was speaking expressively without reservation of his innermost desire to recover his creative glory that he designed in man.

The extent of this love is beyond measure as Paul stated:

> For I am persuaded, that neither death, nor
> life, nor angels, nor principalities, nor powers, nor
> things present, nor things to come, Nor height,
> nor depth, nor any other creature, shall be able
> to separate us from the love of God, which is in
> Christ Jesus our Lord. (Rom. 8:38–39, KJV)

What an awesome God who would go to the extreme of not sparing his own Son to freely give unto us eternal life and the power and privilege to become his children. The heart of God is incomprehensible and bound by an immense immeasurable mystery of love. God so loved us, with an unspeakable joy, his unspeakable gift, of his only begotten Son. His love has proven to be transcendent, and without controversy transparent, and as it never fails in its operation, it is also transforming. The wonder of his love abounds more in more knowledge and understanding as we grow in grace and in the knowledge of the Lord Jesus Christ. His love will continually constrain us as it works in us for his glory. God's love displayed covereth all sins! Oh how we need to grasp the depths of this truth and see who and how those that are guilty of sin, benefit from the display of this love. The disobedient, those that rebel against his word are considered free to come and baste them in this love and receive the richness of his mercy. There is hope for the fool who hath said in his heart there is no God as his love supersedes their unbelief. Those that have despised the glory of God and lack natural affection, burning in their lust for one another, men with men and women with women. Although he has judged their behavior as unseemly and an abomination are covered under the umbrella of this love. He is able to restore truth where a lie has destroyed, light where darkness has blinded. He understands the depth of hurt and degradation of life, the fears and uncertainty that leads to confusion. His love is protective and proactive always abounding in truth with mercy. To the drunkard who is overwhelmed with the issues of life, seeking only rest and peace.

Desiring to have their mind free from all manner of depression and oppression. The love of God beckons them, "Come unto me, all that labour and are heavy laden, and I will give you rest" (Matt. 11:28, KJV) to those who have been captivated by the spirit of lust fulfilling the lust of the flesh and the lust of the mind. Driven by pornography, obsessed with sexual pleasure, full of fornication and adultery. Worshipping the creature more than the Creator. He cries out to them, look unto me and live and the life I will give unto you will be abundant.

There is no one exempt from this everlasting love, no one beyond its reach, no one unworthy its amazing grace. It reaches to the uttermost areas of life defile by sins destructive force. It is capable of covering the perversions of those lured by child pornography, able to forbear the violent murderer and the most ruthless acts of evil. This loves exceeds the boundaries of nations and cultures, overcomes idolatry, witchcraft, and all manner of satanic worship. Those full of pride and arrogant in their ways are yet within the scope of this compassing love. This love can soften the harden heart; revive the wounded, bitter, and broken. It reaches the rich and the poor alike, the tormented, afflicted and even the possessed. God displayed his love to reach the unreachable, to covet the undesirable, to deliver the miserable. The Love of God was displayed in his forbearance of sin until the fullness of times was come when God brought forth his Son. This matchless love has forever been destined to bring forth the reconciliation of God and man.

> In this was manifested the love of God
> toward us, because that God sent his only
> begotten Son into the world, that we might live

through him. Herein is love, not that we loved
God, but that he loved us, and sent his son to
be the propitiation for our sins. (1 John 4:9–10,
KJV)

Man has been at enmity with God and has proven his unwill-
ingness to love him, Oh! Bless the LORD for the atonement that has
absorbed all the bruises thereof. And now the loves of God has been
openly displayed and pour out abundantly upon us independent
of any love for him. Love and justice has brought us to the cross
of Christ forever satisfying the wrath and judgment of God. The
greatness of this love does not just cover all sin past, present, and
future, it also covers sin everywhere. God so loved the world! Every
nation, every tongue, every culture has been designated as recipients.
All humanity is God's mission field and he has commissioned the
church to do his bidding.

Go ye therefore and teach all nations, bap-
tizing them in the name of the Father, and of the
Son, and of the Holy Ghost: Teaching them to
observe all things whatsoever I have commanded
you: and, lo, I am with you always, even unto the
end of the world. Amen. (Matt. 28:19–20, KJV)

All over the entire world there are countless belief systems.
Every man born in the flesh has been charged by God to look unto
Jesus. Look away from their thoughts about God. Trust not in their
own understanding as they perceive. That which they have come to
reasonably believe to be true about God, learn to weigh it against the
claims of Christ who said, "I am the way, the truth, and the life: no
man cometh unto God but by me (John 14:6, KJV). Who spoke the
world into existence, who calls those things that are not as though
they are, who was manifested in the flesh to taste death for every
man and destroy him who had the power of death, the devil. Who

was crucified and rose from the grave the third day according to the scriptures.

> Who being in the form of God thought it not robbery to be equal with God: But made himself of no reputation, and took upon him the form of a servant, and was made in the likeness of men. And being found in fashion as a man, humbled himself, and became obedient unto death, even the death of the cross. (Phil. 2:6–8, KJV)

To the uttermost parts of the earth, God has proclaimed that his love is the greatest of all and warrants that all men everywhere to take heed to it. No one has ever given there only begotten son to pay the debt for the sin of others. No one has been so willing to suffer the abuse of sinners and yet lovingly say with passion, "Father, forgive them for they know not what they do." To the east and the west, the north and the south, go into the highways and byways and compel men to come. The earth belongs unto the Lord and with good reason all that therein is. He has taken the responsibility upon himself to preserve his word throughout history and execute his judgments from one generation to the next. That all men everywhere may have the opportunity to set their hearts right with God. There are no merits or works that can be done on the behalf of humanity that will satisfy the righteous demands of God. He has set the standard for all men to see, and that standard is Christ. No imagination or presumptuous thoughts about God can meet his approval for justification. The only way to God is the way he has displayed.

> Enter ye in at the strait gate: for wide is the gate, and broad is the way, that leadeth to destruction, and many there be which go in there at: Because strait is the gate, and narrow is the way, which leadeth unto life, and few there be that find it. (Matt. 7:13–14, KJV)

He has displayed his love in such a fashion that whosoever will believe in him shall not perish but have everlasting life. Consider the scope of his providence that as all are guilty and fall short, all will be without excuse that refuses to believe him. The entire world is guilty before him with whom we have to do. The truth that has been relative to the history and experiences of all nations and cultures, everyone everywhere is bought subject to Divine Truth. Regardless of how fully persuaded one may be of their particular view of God, from their traditions, culture, religion or even their own judgments: they will still have to surrender them to Jesus Christ. He alone is the manifestation of the love of God placed on display.

> Wherefore God also hath highly exalted him, and given him a name which is above every name: That at the name of Jesus every knee should bow, of things in heaven, and things in earth, and things under the earth; And that every tongue should confess that Jesus Christ is Lord, to the glory of God the Father. (Phil. 2:9–11, KJV)

This is not some old wives fable or fairy tale, this the distinct accounting of the testimony that God has given to all mankind about his only begotten Son. All others are mere opinions about what they perceive to be truth, or at best a diluted version of partial truth. But God has put on display his great love and boldly proclaims the truth of it based upon the death, burial and resurrection of his Son. This truth is so profound that it presents two ends, believe it and you will not perish or refuse to believe it and perish. God is not like man that he should lie. He has been consistent with himself throughout eternity: It is impossible for him to lie! So shall my word be that goeth forth out of my mouth: it shall not return unto me void, but it shall accomplish that which I please, and it shall proper in the thing whereto I sent it (Isa. 55:11, KJV). The love of God is broader than the scope of our transgressions his word displays. It was by his word that all these things have been accomplished as he sent forth his word to validate his love. "Thus said the Lord, in the beginning was the Word and, and the Word was with God, and the Word was GOD" (John 1:11, KJV). "God is love" (1 John 4:8b). "And the Word was made flesh, and dwelt among us, and we beheld his glory, the glory as of the only begotten of the Father, full of grace and truth" (John 1:14, KJV). According to the scriptures, God has magnified his word above his name.

The love of God is displayed by God humbling himself, giving his Son as a sacrifice in our place, and raising him from the dead, enabling him to freely give everlasting life to whoever comes to him by faith to receive it. The plan of redeeming man from sin and death was intended that we should be to the praise of his glory, who trusted in Christ. In whom after trusting, after hearing and believing the word of truth of the gospel. Were sealed with the holy spirit of promise, which is the earnest of our inheritance until the redemption of the purchased possession, unto the praise of his glory (Eph. 1:12–14, KJV, paraphrased). The love of God that was displayed signed, sealed, and delivered all the components that would provide for man's present peace and joy, and eternal assurance as children of God. God is the progenitor of family. It is his will to create and establish the family of God. But as many as received him, to them gave the power to become the children of God, even to them that believe on his name. Which were born, not of blood, nor of the will of the flesh, nor of the will of man, but of God. (John 1:12–13, KJV, paraphrased). Let us be clear here the God of heaven and earth in the riches of his grace, by his matchless wisdom and foreknowledge, purposed in his heart to make humanity an intimate part of his family. What a divine honor that ranks to none for that which was made from the dust of the earth! What glorious and magnificent display of loving-kindness bestowed upon man who has been at enmity with God! No man has the power to position himself in such a relationship with God on his own merits. No man would even know how to obtain such privilege that he could even approach the Most High God with even the thought to be considered. The love of God displayed and the blessings that are connected with it by this spirit of adoption is now a legally binding covenant through the mercy of God. As a wise master builder, God has laid a sure foundation for all to see and partake of that will enable them to grow and know more truth as they approach the work of God on his terms. His terms have been defined by the love that he displayed.

God so loved the world that whosoever believe. Again, it is to our advantage to take the instructions that God has defined for us to come to know the truth. The means that God has determined to be utilized to receive the benefits he has prepared for all is faith. Faith is not a natural action that we just utilize. God has chosen faith to bring men back to the place he originally designed, to trust and obey his word. So then faith cometh by hearing and hearing by the word of God (Rom. 10:17, KJV). The simplicity and truth that God has conveyed is also the most challenging for man to submit to. It deprives man of any ability to do anything that he can take and claim for his own justification. The faith that is required is not just an act of believing anything, but believing specifically what and how the gospel message proclaims.

> That if thou shalt confess with thy mouth the Lord Jesus, and shalt believe in thine heart that God hath raised him from the dead, thou shalt be saved. For with the heart man believeth unto righteousness; and with the mouth confession is made unto salvation. (Rom. 10:9–10, KJV)

This is the core substance of the call of God, in his display of love, that all would be obedient to the faith of the gospel of the Lord Jesus Christ. The death, burial, and resurrection of the Lord Jesus Christ is the substance of the word of God. The death, burial, and resurrection of the Lord Jesus Christ is the epitome of the love of God displayed, for the whole world to see and believe. How dependent God would have us be upon his word? How often we have failed to recognize the sovereign right of God to mandate and instruct. The voice of the Lord has spoken that he has displayed his love. Our hearing needs to be overhauled that all of the multitudes of voices that fight to enter our hearing may be silenced, that we might have an ear to hear and obey the word of God. Today, we can honestly say that we were not there, and we did not see him or this display of love. But be advised those that do believe would gladly testify of him: "Whom having not seen, ye love; in whom, though now ye see him not, yet believing, ye rejoice with joy unspeakable and full of glory; Receiving the end of your faith, even the salvation of your souls" (1 Pet. 1:8–9, KJV). We would see Jesus!

12

God's Love Rejected

He that believeth on the Son of God
hath the witness in himself:
he that believeth not God hath made
him a liar; because he believeth
not the record that God gave his Son.

—1 John 5:10 (KJV)

In the play *Hamlet*, the question arose that created a dialogue about life and death, and the question was, "To be or not to be?" That is the question as *Hamlet* would contemplate the fears of death versus the ills of life. However, he used this line of questioning to analyze his own questions, thoughts, and fears about suicide. We need to consider the reality of the question and the consequences of "to believe or not to believe?" At this place of contemplation, I submit to you the reality of not believing, for not to believe would be none less than rejecting the love of God. We will revisit the reality of believing in our concluding chapter. It may seem a bit odd to refer to *Hamlet* as he was considering suicide and struggled with his conscience, believing that suicide was a crime in the eyes of God. But I boldly proclaim to you on this occasion without reservation that for you not to believe is as the crime of suicide before God. We live and die and life goes on, day by day, year after year; we see things as they are, and in some cases things that change, and in many cases things remain the same. The ills of life and our views of God affect what we do and also what we do not do. Oftentimes, we think that God is not concern or that he is not involved with the affairs of mankind and is inactive. "The Lord is not slack concerning his promise, as some men count slackness; but is long-suffering to us-ward, not willing that any should perish, but that all should come to repentance" (2 Pet. 3:9, KJV). God is patient in his dealing with man considering the work of the cross sufficient to give grace to allow man to call upon him.

The forbearance of God is intentional, for his compassion and tender mercies are new every morning with the aim of showing that he is not willing that any should perish. The love of God is a display of mercy and truth kissing each other meeting man at his point of need with resolve. Therefore, for anyone to be hard-hearted and reject the love of God is a deliberate act of self-termination by not claiming God's gift of love for themselves. God's judgment is based upon truth, for one to despise the grace of God and count the precious blood of Jesus that was shed for the forgiveness of sin, as something to be trampled under the feet, sign their own doom. God is made a liar to one who chooses not to believe the record he gave his Son. Such an indictment on God, who has provided us with such a great salvation, propels one to be full of calamity leading to ruin. What is involved with the indictment upon God that judges him as a liar? Primarily, it is an assault on the nature, being, and character of a holy God. It is a railing accusation from the depths of resentment, rebellion, and bitterness toward all he represents. To suggest that Jesus Christ was not born of a virgin, was not 100 percent God and 100 percent man, that he did not do the miracles that he claimed, did not willingly lay down his life on the cross of Calvary for the sins of all mankind, and finally on the third day did not rise from the grave.

Furthermore, that none of these actions were done because God genuinely loves you and me. It is a strong suggestion that their thoughts are greater than God's thoughts and their judgments have more validity than that which the Bible conveys to be true about God. This indictment and claim unfortunately many adhere to, and to them, it is all just a lie and has no significance. They are those who are full of pride and in their arrogance resist the truth and all that God has declared to be true about himself. They are those who, through too much knowledge, become puffed up and think higher of themselves than they ought. They are those that in their own ignorance and foolishness say in their hearts there is no God. They are those who have become fully persuaded of other droughts about idols, gods, and other religions that compel them to resist the truth. Whatever the motive or the cause, they all fall under the judgment of unbelief.

"He that believeth on him is not condemned: but he that believeth not is condemned already, because he hath not believed in the name of the only begotten Son of God" (John 3:18, KJV). What is meant here by being condemned already? The only way man can come to know truth about God is by means of God himself revealing it. Therefore, for one to reject revealed truth places him under the condemnation of God, for choosing to disregard God's revelation. It is God who has said all have sinned and fall short of the glory of God. God said, "The wages of sin is death." Man who refuses to accept and submit to the truth that God has made known remains in the state of death destined to eternal damnation. For in the beginning, God judged in the day that Adam disobeyed the voice and instruction of God, ye shall surely die. Death was sure and certain, spiritual death was an immediate judgment with physical death to be inevitable. To be condemned is to be sentenced to be punished; in this particular case, the punishment is death. One of the consequences of death is alienation from God. This separation is more tragic than many come to realize. There is no fellowship with light and darkness! The scriptures have concluded, "God is light and in Him is no darkness at all" (1 John 1:5, KJV). The sun has been identified as the main source of light and heat that affects every process of life on the earth, in the waters and even under the earth. The plants receive the proper amount of light and heat from it, all of mankind; it powers all life from insects to the fish in the sea. There is a necessity for light for all creation to function naturally. Likewise and even more so spiritually, God is the source of spiritual life and all the process of it. He has set himself apart from all others being the only self-sufficient being that exist. Everyone and everything is dependent on him alone. So, to be alienated and separated from him is death.

The death of Jesus Christ was proven to be the death that would forever satisfy the judgment of death. On the cross of Calvary Jesus was hanging, beaten and bruised, with his hands and feet pierced, suffering agony beyond comprehension. The Son of God, despised and rejected of men, looks up to heaven and speaks eternal love that passeth understanding, "Father forgive them, for they know not what they do" (Luke 23:34, KJV). The forgiveness of sins is the grounds that the love of God is dispersed on. The love of God is not overwhelmed by the hatred that man shows toward him. As a matter of fact, the scriptures proclaim that the natural minded man hates God and is not subject to the law of God because they that are in the flesh cannot please God. Consider this amazing love wherein he loves us with, reaching the most defiled with mercy untold. He is alive today interceding before God the Father that he might grant them repentance, that they might be saved and come into the knowledge of the truth. Jesus is able to have compassion being touched with the infirmities of all and likewise being familiar with their temptations. His long-suffering and forbearance will only go but to an appointed time, where all have an appointment with death. "Whereas ye know not what shall be on tomorrow. For what is your life? It is even a vapour that appeareth for a little time, and then vanisheth away" (James 4:14, KJV). Tomorrow is not promised. All we can account for is today, for yesterday is gone never to return again. Therefore, it behooves you to examine the claims of the love of God in sincerity and truth, not in presumption and ignorance. The apostle Paul was no stranger to the experience from the depravity and darkness of sin, for he tells us of his testimony.

> And I thank Christ Jesus our Lord, who hath enabled me, putting me into the ministry; Who was before a blasphemer, and a persecutor, and injurious: but I obtained mercy, because I did it ignorantly in unbelief. And the grace of our Lord was exceeding abundant with faith in love which is in Christ Jesus. This is a faithful saying,

and worthy of all acceptation, that Christ Jesus
came into the world to save sinners; of whom I
am chief. (1 Tim. 1:12–15, KJV)

God knows your ignorance of him in truth; he sees your unbelief, fear and doubt, and can even deliver you from your blasphemy
toward his name. Looking closely at Paul the sinner before he came
to Christ he resisted the truth, was committed to murdering anyone who believed that Jesus was the Christ the Son of the Living
God, and furthermore, he was guilty of blasphemy. Who would have
known that this would be the character of the man God would use
to write most of the New Testament scriptures. The wisdom of God
is matchless when you intelligently examine his heart's desire to persuade men of the love of God to the extent that he uses someone
who considers himself the chief of sinners. To reject the love of God
after coming into the knowledge of the truth will be as crucifying the
Lord Jesus Christ again and counting it as nothing. Here is evidence
of things to hope for if you feel it is too hard for you to come to God,
or even to be able to receive his love. There is nothing too hard for
God even when it is impossible for man.

Unbelief has been the demise of man in his relationship with
God as he has failed to respond to God on his terms. Looking at God
at work in Israel, we can see how this would be a testimony against
them. Time and time again, God would rise up prophets and gave
them his word to instruct them and in their unbelief, they rebelled
against his word. Rejecting his counsel and choosing to lean to their
own understanding and pursuing their own desires. God's work in
the nation of Israel teaches us how they also rejected the love of God
and would suffer the consequences thereof. The Lord said:

O Jerusalem, Jerusalem, who kills the
prophets and stones those sent to her, how often
I have longed to gather your children together,
as a hen gathers her chickens and ye would not.
Behold your house left unto you desolate. (Matt.
23:37–38, KJV)

The affection displayed here by a mother hen protecting her chicks is with strong passion and affection. The metaphor here typifies even the love of God for his Children Israel desiring to cover them from all harm as he sends out alarms of pending danger. However, history records Israel killing the prophets, rebelling against God and suffering the consequences. The indictment on God that he is liar is seen displayed in history in the hearts of man from one generation to the next. Man, in his vanity and foolishness, has exalted his thoughts and imaginations to often above the word of God. Yet the word of God remains true, and it accomplishes what God intended.

God has consistently expressed his thoughts and affections towards the children of Israel and it exemplify his thoughts toward us today; according to his promise that all the families of the earth would be blessed through them, because of the covenant that he made with Abraham. God has said, "For I know the thoughts that I think toward you, saith the LORD, thoughts of peace, not of evil, to give you an expected end" (Jer. 29:11, KJV). God knows and purpose in his heart to make known the riches of his grace and mercy through Christ Jesus. He is the unspeakable gift of the love of God manifest in the flesh. God knows how frail we are, remembering that we are but dust, so he is being touched with our infirmities is always willing to intercede on our behalf. There is no depth that he cannot reach nor individual that he careth not for. It is such a sad reality that such darkness and hardness of heart and mind hinders man from humbling himself to reach the boundless love of God reserved for whosoever will.

> And this is the condemnation that the light
> has come into the world, and men loved darkness
> rather than light, because their deeds were evil.
> For everyone that doeth evil hateth the light, nei-
> ther cometh to the light, lest his deeds should be
> reproved. (John 3:19–20, KJV)

The light and truth of God exposes man to see what and how they really are. All are naked before him and nothing is hidden. The light of the gospel truth exposes the ignorance, foolishness, and vanity of man that unfortunately he is in bondage to. He has chosen to set his affections on the things of darkness declining to receive the reproofs of Christ that are contrary to the ungodliness of their ways. Such rejection of the ministry of grace deprives themselves from seeing the manifestation of his glory. Oh! That man would praise God's goodness and his wonderful works toward the children of men. To believe or not to believe? That is the question. How eternally full of darkness, death, and damnation awaits those who believe not. There is no recourse of recovery, only a continuous never-ending grip in the claws of torment and unimaginable deprivation under the wrath of God. There is but one way to be subject to such alienation from the True and Living God and that is to reject his love. You and you alone can deliver yourself from the pending eternal condemnation designated only to those who reject the love of God. Yes, it is as the sin of suicide to fail to hasten to the everlasting love of God full of grace and truth, mercy, and loving-kindness. None other has loved so dearly, none other can provide so entirely, none other can protect so assuredly. His love is by choice not that we chose God, but he has chosen us.

> According as he hath chosen us in him before the foundation of the world, that we should be holy and without blame before him in love. Having predestined us unto the adoption of children by Jesus Christ to himself according to the good pleasure of his will. (Eph. 1:4–5, KJV)

This was not a mere coincidence that just happened in the history of mankind. God purposed to show all humanity the riches of his grace and loving-kindness through Christ Jesus before the foundation of the world. His thoughts toward us have been innumerable and with good intentions. It is inconceivable in the finite mind of man that such a thing could be, but praise be unto the Most High God that he is not like man. To reject the love of God is to go deliberately against the good pleasure of his will.

God said unto the Children of Israel:

> I call heaven and earth to record this day against you, that I have set before your life and death, blessing and cursing: therefore choose life, that both thou and thy seed may live: that thou mayest love the LORD thy God, and that thou mayest obey his voice, and that thou cleave unto him: for he is thy life, and the length of thy days. (Deut. 30:19–20, KJV)

God is pleased with his desire to deliver and save man from his own wrath. He is pleased to provide an eternal covenant to commit himself to on your behalf. He is pleased to satisfy his righteous judgment and make you accepted in and by his beloved Son Jesus Christ. It is the good pleasure of his will for you to choose life and not death. God has brought man to and continually brings man to the valley of decision. He has worked both the will, and the do, of his good pleasure, all that is required of you is to choose to believe and obey. It is sad and unfortunate that we have such a negative view of God and obedience to him, but God has provided for us all the resources necessary to meet the high calling of God in Christ Jesus. Because God is jealous for you, he has taken full responsibility for all things that pertain to life and godliness making you accepted in the beloved. The power to transform from darkness to light, from death to life is but in an act of faith in what he has said. I speak as a fool, if it were possible for God to lie, he would have nothing to gain by saving wretched sinners from his wrath who rebel against his will. But because it is impossible for him to lie, he has given all of himself to regain and restore the glory, honor, and image that he intended when he first uttered the words, "Let us make man in our image, after our likeness and let them have dominion" (Gen. 1:26, KJV).

13

What Manner of Love Is This?

*Behold what manner of love the
Father hath bestowed upon us,
That we should be called the sons
of God; therefore the world
knoweth us not because it knew him not.*

—1 John 3:1 (KJV)

The awe and wonder that we should fix our hearts upon the love of God is here highly appreciated. Let us fix our eyes upon it to look intently at the magnificence of it and what it has done for us. Let us exercise and direct our affections toward it that we may be overwhelmed by it. Let it demand our attention like none other that we may lavish in the benefits of it. There is no one like God, no one can love so immensely, and that enriches and exalts one to be in such a relationship that he would call you his children. We who by nature have been disobedient, having no merit of our own, filled with disdain, unworthiness and all manner of ungodliness, he hath chosen to adopt. We are here exhorted to take care to set a high value on our view of the love of God toward us. This extraordinary love that is boundless with widths, lengths, depths and heights untold, that passeth knowledge is a Divine love. This love gives us just cause to pray, "Our Father which art in heaven hallowed be thy name!" Hallowed be thy name for giving us the privilege to call you Father and finding ourselves worthy to be called thy children. He is worthy of our adoration and praise and that without reservation. The type of adoration that he deserves is exemplified in the scriptures.

> And behold, a woman in the city, which was a sinner, when she knew Jesus sat at meat in the Pharisee's house, brought an alabaster box of ointment, And stood at his feet weeping, and began to wash his feet with tears, and did wipe them with the hairs of her head, and kissed his feet, and anointed them with ointment. (Luke 7:37–38, KJV)

Our response to his love should spill out of us in such gratitude that everything we do offers a sweet scent of worship and praise with thanksgiving.

Her adoration of the Savior was fueled by her humility as she offered her sacrifice of praise and worship. Her tears were plentiful as they embraced the fact that the forgiveness of sin was not to be taken lightly as a common thing for now she is free. Free to live from the bondage that held her captive to sin and death. She is able to behold him and recognize he alone is worthy so she washes his feet with her tears. What a beautiful picture of sincerity and truth in her worship, with tender loving care. The value she placed on the opportunity alone to be in his presence was displayed, and she used every moment. Free to approach him who is unapproachable lest he beckons you to come. She adorns his feet with kisses as she establishes herself in the fear of the LORD. This is the mark of those who have been raptured by such a manner of love as this. Rarely do we see such a vivid illustration of a sinner who has earnestly submitted themselves to the love of God. These are the type of examples that convey our utmost desire to show him love and affection and his highest praise.

It is to be understood that the alabaster box of ointment is so precious and valuable that it is the very last thing mentioned. It could easily be said she saved the best for last. This expensive perfume was a type of us presenting our lives as a living sacrifice broken and pour out so that all that God has placed in us through Christ can come out. Christ in us is the hope of glory and the pure and undefiled precious ointment that is contained on the inside. Once broken, we would have access to the priceless ointment of the life of Christ that we can go into all the world and tell others of the good news. "How beautiful are the feet of them that preach the gospel of peace, and bring glad tidings of good things!" (Rom. 10:15b, KJV). Jesus himself washed the disciple's feet suggesting that they do the same to each other as an expression of love and humility of mind and spirit. The character of Christ has been magnified in serving in the lowest of all places. The washing of feet was considered the lowliest of all jobs performed primarily by slaves. It is but our reasonable service to offer our bodies to him as our praise and worship. She used the ointment to anoint the Savior's feet; I can only begin to state with little insight on how much this typifies the benefits of this manner of love. The broken and contrite spirit that gives itself wholeheartedly to serve the Lord will find themselves elevated to be no longer servants but adopted children and heirs. What God has placed within us in Christ is built upon a better covenant with better promises that have everlasting value giving us an inheritance making us joint heirs with Christ. "For both he that sanctifieth and they who are sanctified is all of one: for which cause he is not ashamed to call them brethren" (Heb. 2:11, KJV).

We, by our very nature, have been in bondage through the fear of death all of our lifetime in this flesh. But God by an operation made without hands translated us into his Son representing the spirit of adoption. Clothing us with all the rights and privileges to be part of the eternal family of God. Even so we, when we were children, were in bondage under the elements of the world:

> But when the fullness of the time was come,
> God sent forth his Son, made of a woman, made
> under the law, to redeem them that were under
> the law, that we might receive the adoption of

> sons, And because ye are sons, God hath sent
> forth the Spirit of his Son into your hearts crying,
> Abba Father. Wherefore thou art no more a ser-
> vant, but a son, then heir of God through Christ.
> (Gal. 4:3–6, KJV)

This is the work of God's hands that he performed then enabled us to be partakers of. God himself has literally taken us from being servants to becoming children. The significance of this transition of position is cause for so much joy and exhilaration. The change of relationship makes all the difference in the world and we need to grasp it. What can compare to being called and having the everlasting position as a child of the Most High God forever.

The love of God has forever secured for us the right to son-ship, and the work of God that went into the process is more than phenomenal.

> And you, that were sometime alienated and
> enemies in your mind by wicked works, yet now
> hath he reconciled in the body of his flesh through
> death, to present you holy and unblameable and
> unreprovable in his sight. (Col. 1:21–22, KJV)

We cannot overlook the fact that God is a Holy God and cannot be defiled. He has recreated new life through the redemption work of the cross of Calvary. The plan of redemption was a complete work of salvation involving the entire scope of the needs of God and man. We understand that God so loved the world that he gave his only begotten Son. But it is the *what* and *how* of the plan that reveals the intricate details of this great salvation. This aspect of the work of God has been defined as a mystery because it has all been done in Christ. To discover what is behind and involved in this manner of love here is where we begin. What is the mystery of Christ? That their hearts might be comforted being knit together in love and unto all riches of the full assurance of understanding, to the acknowledgment of the mystery of God, and of the Father, and of Christ; in whom are hid all the treasures of wisdom and knowledge (Col. 2:2–3, KJV). The deep things of God are not clearly seen for they come only by revelation. The apostle Paul was blessed by God not only to see the deep things that God had purpose to do in Christ, but he also was given the responsibility to make them known writing most of the New Testament scriptures.

What God purposed in his heart was to reconcile all things unto himself by the death, burial, and resurrection of Jesus Christ. In Christ, God was satisfying his need to execute his righteous judgment that went forth out of his mouth in the beginning. In Christ, God fulfilled the prophecy foretold in the Old Testament concerning him coming in the flesh to make the presence of God known with man. In Christ, God was fulfilling each and every demand of his commandments leaving known undone. In Christ, God was making peace with man on his terms with the understanding that he would be just and the justifier of those who would believe in him. In Christ, God created a new man that would be the expressed image of his person so that his word would not return unto him void, concluding that his creation of man was very good. In Christ, God would destroy the works of the devil and deliver man from being subject to his vile works and the power of death. In Christ, God satisfied every need that man had that kept him from obeying and loving the Lord with all their heart, mind, and strength. How did he accomplish all of these things?

> Giving thanks unto the Father, which hath made us meet to be partakers of the inheritance of the saints in light: Who hath delivered us from the power of darkness, and hath translated us into the kingdom of his dear Son: In whom we have redemption through his blood, even the forgiveness of sins. (Col. 1:12–14, KJV)

He is God Almighty able to create, deliver, translate, transform, make, and remake, tear down and build up, all according to what he purposed. For it is he who hath made us and not us ourselves, for he is the potter and we are but clay.

Only to those that through faith in the finished work of redemption can one become a child of God and with this knowledge of truth comes consequences. We are now able to understand the reality of how the world does not know God and likewise not able to know the truth that is in us. Now that the eyes of our understanding are open after having come into the knowledge of the truth, we must walk in the fear of the LORD. Having respect unto his word and whole counsel that we might be transformed by it. Now we are the children of God by this great love wherein he hath loved us with. It is beyond our ability to limit the power of it, but we can deprive our self of realizing its truth and experiencing that practical application of its power. The power of this love is what brought forth the resurrection of Jesus Christ and has also raised us up in him. Therefore, we are admonished by this same love.

> If ye then be risen with Christ; seek those things which are above, where Christ sitteth on the right hand of God. Set your affection on things above not on things on the earth. For ye are dead, and your life is bid with Christ in God. (Col. 3:1–3, KJV)

This too is also part of the mystery that God has made known unto us and the glory of it that makes this manner of love work in us mightily. Mighty to sanctify us wholly body, soul, and spirit in this life that we may walk in him by faith in love. Thus Jesus prayed to this end. "Holy Father, sanctify them through thy truth: thy word is truth. As thou hast sent me into the world, even so have I also sent them into the world. And for their sake I sanctify myself, that they also might be sanctified through the truth" (John 17:17–19, KJV). The transforming power of the love of God is at work purging within all that is not like Christ, exposing all that is dark, and bringing it to the light. The ground for the love of God to be most effective on is truth. God is diligent and willing to teach line upon line, precept upon precept those who desire to know truth.

Our desire is the most precious commodity that we have and we are so vulnerable to not having any or losing what little we have for the things of God. We desire some of everything and are never satisfied yet we continue to desire. Oh! But to just taste and see for yourself the goodness of the Lord and his love for you, you will never be the same. For to allow the Lord himself to be the desire of your heart, your satisfaction will be abundant and overflowing because of his love. As newborn babes, desire the sincere milk of the word that ye may grow thereby: If so be ye have tasted that the Lord is gracious (1 Pet. 2:23, KJV). This manner of love that God has bestowed on us is holy. The truth of the word of God is living and powerful able to work in us the character of his love. God's desire is to sanctify us by the truth of his word that we may be partakers of the divine nature. God is a holy God and to be able to share in his nature is a benefit that compliments his love. Holiness is the aim and destination for man that God has determined to bring glory and honor to his name. Be ye holy for I am holy, this love is perfect and ensures the bond of perfectness in those that believe. The mind of Christ is devoted to see that the same love that God loved the Son with be in those that is called to be the children of God.

How does God work such a great work within sinful man that he has exalted by this love to eternal glory?

> And I will pray the father and he shall give you another Comforter that he may abide with you forever; Even the Spirit of truth whom the world cannot receive, because it seeth him not, neither knoweth him: but ye know him: for he dwelleth with you, and shall be in you. (John14:16–17, KJV)

To us, it may seem to be mysterious, but to God, the person and work of the Holy Spirit is mandatory. He is the authorized agent that God has chosen to use to implement all of his objectives in man and in the earth. When Jesus prayed for the Father to send another Comforter, he was positioning him to come and execute, enact, and enforce all that he accomplished in his redemptive work. The matchless wisdom of God is here manifested to go beyond any and every need that man will have so that he can work both the will and the ability to do them. This is the testimony of God making himself known through the Holy Spirit to be all sufficient that in nothing grace would be lacking. What manner of love is this that God has bestowed upon us that he would not spare his only begotten Son, give us exceeding great and precious promises, make an eternal covenant with us, adopt us into his family, and give us another comforter to be in us and with us. This love is worthy of us being overwhelmed and full of awe and wonder. The Holy Spirit is that comforter; he is the spirit of truth designated to convince us of sin, judgment, and righteousness.

What shall we then say to these things? If God be for us, who shall be against us? (Rom. 8:31, KJV). This manner of love proves with many infallible proofs that God is for us. This manner of love is without question beyond anything we could conceive in our thoughts. This manner of love is far reaching in its scope and able to save to the uttermost. This manner of love believes all things, hopes in all things, and never fails. If anyone were to really experience this manner of love for themselves, they will immediately surrender all. Being lost but now are found, blind but now see, bound but now made free, guilty yet now forever justified, enemies of God now adopted in the beloved. If these things be true, (I speak this with reservation knowing that it is a fact) we should have our hearts filled with gratitude, our minds set to seek and learn to know and understand all truth, our affections yielded to this love, our mouth filled with praise, and our will give to obey. There is no greater love than this and to realize that it is coming from the God of heaven and earth makes it magnificent whomsoever will let him come and behold what manner of love is this that saves and makes whole. Be ever mindful of this amazing grace and rich mercy that has been pouring out for all to receive.

For God so loved the world that he gave his only begotten Son, that whosoever believeth in him should not perish, but have everlasting life. For God sent not his Son into the world to condemn the world; but that the world through him might be saved. (John 3:16–17, KJV)

This is the manner of love that God has bestowed upon, never to be condemning but to be made into the image of his Son.

14

The Beseeching of God

Now then we are ambassadors
for Christ, as though God
did beseech you by us: we pray
you in Christ's stead, be ye
reconciled to God.

—2 Corinthians 5:20 (KJV)

As much as is within me to share with you the burden and utmost concern of my heart, I pray that you would at least listen to my admonishment to you with some curiosity. It is my passion and desire to see all men come to Christ and be spared the wrath of God; however, it is not within my ability to make anyone do anything.

> For we must all appear before the judgment seat of Christ: that every one may receive the things done in the body according to that he hath done, whether it be good or bad. Knowing therefore the terror of the Lord, we persuade men. (2 Cor. 5:10–11a, KJV)

Please understand for God to suggest that he is beseeching you, that is urgently imploring you, it could be said knowing the fate of those that would deny the Christ, he is literally begging you to not put yourself in that position against his judgment. The following arguments I present to you are designed to persuade you to examine yourself in the light of what you believe to be true against the claims of Jesus Christ as the personification of truth, and the only way for anyone to come to know God, as well as the only means by which anyone can be righteous before God. Let's be clear here you and I both know, no one knows you better than your own ability to make an honest assessment of yourself, but God. No one knows the secrets of your heart and why you think and judge the issues of life the way you do, but God. No one can say that your feelings are not genuine and true and have become a part of how you view and experienced life, the issues thereof, and God. To be able to determine what is right and wrong in our own eyes seem to be the most acceptable norm of things. I submit to you three fundamental arguments about God for your consideration, ideological, practical, and spiritual.

Ideological argument: It has been determined that there are approximately 7.12 billion people on the face of the earth. That could also represent potentially the same amount of views or ideas about God. If you consider that as a possibility, it would be mind boggling! God has given us the entire greatest asset in the world—the mind. It has been examined and studied for centuries and the conclusion has been that it is the most fascinating and the most powerful tool known to mankind. That being said, it should not be a difficult thing for one to conceive that our thoughts and ideas, however, plenteous they maybe could be right or wrong. Some may say that it is relative what you consider to be true or false, right or wrong. But let us examine this thought with a higher regard for our lack of knowledge since we are so prone to be presumptuous especially in matters that we know that are pass finding out. It would be foolish for me to proclaim that I know all there is to know about God. Likewise, it would be just as foolish for me to fail to attempt to inform all that would hear, that which he has made known about himself. There are only two means wherein we formulate our belief systems by, through history or by that which we create in our own minds. Historically speaking, there are countless belief systems that has been passed down from one generation to the next through cultures, religions, philosophy, and various ideologies. Then there is the vast capacity for one to soar the reins of the imagination fueled by their own self will.

We all filter our belief systems through one of these two means. However, we choose to formulate what we believe. It is imperative that we consider the claims of Jesus Christ in relation to what we believe. Why should you? If what Jesus Christ said of himself is true, then it is impossible for anything else to live up to the grounds of truth. He has set himself apart from all other thoughts and views about God in three vitally important aspects. First, in the virgin birth. We can say what we will about this miracle but the fact of the matter is only God could claim and execute such a wonder as this. Second, he declares himself alone to be the way the truth and the life for all mankind to come to God. Third and most importantly, he said to his disciples,

> Behold, we go up to Jerusalem; and the Son of man shall be betrayed unto the chief priests and unto the scribes, and they shall condemn him to death, And shall deliver him to the Gentiles to mock, and scourge, and to crucify him: and the third day he shall rise again. (Matt. 20:18–19, KJV)

The death, burial, and resurrection are the foundation of the gospel of Jesus Christ, but if he never rose from the dead, then faith in him and his work is vain. Death, for all practical purposes, is the enemy of man; Christ alone has risen from the dead.

When God created man, it was never his intention for man to die. Unfortunately seeing that it was a judgment of God upon man, we have for all our existence accepted death as the norm of life. But just think for a moment how futile it is just to live for the only purpose to die. God designed man in his image to live forever that is why when Jesus came to satisfy God's judgment of death for every one born of the flesh, it was boldly proclaimed. For God so loved the world that he gave his only begotten Son, that whosoever believeth in him shall not perish but have everlasting life. Everlasting life is the will of God and has been from the creation of man. But here is the significant factor; God could not allow man to live forever in a sinful state, which is also the reason that Jesus took upon himself sinful flesh that he might take away the sin of the world. There is no religion, no ideology, no philosophy, and no self-made realization that could accomplish that. We all have an appointment with death no matter what culture, no matter what country, no matter what ideology, no matter what belief system. Only Jesus Christ has the authority to give eternal life. Jesus said, "I am the resurrection, and the life he that believeth in me, though he were dead, yet shall he live: And whosoever liveth and believeth in me shall never die. Believest thou this?" (John 11:25–26, KJV). Again, this is the claims of the only one who loves you more than you love yourself and has proven it with his life. No one or no other god has made such claims and validated it with their own life; for there is no other god and it is impossible with man. Based upon this argument, I beseech you in God's stead, be ye reconciled to God!

Practical argument: "As it is written, there is none righteous, no not one, there is none that understandeth, and there is none that seeketh after God" (Rom. 3:10–11, KJV). In these words alone, we must conclude all mankind under the judgment of sin. God has judged all of humanity as not being interested in him in sincerity and truth enough to seek to know him. Because of this lack of knowledge, he concludes also that there is none that understands the truth about him. Furthermore, any and all of man's best efforts to obtain any resemblance of righteousness is futile from his perspective and standards. One of the questions in life that has plagued mankind is centered around "the problem of evil." What a tremendous amount of confusion, frustration, and uncertainty has been experienced with the thoughts associated with this question. Truly, this has been one of the questions of man that is beyond his own capacity to find out the answer. How is it logically possible for God and evil to coexist and God being good? But God and only God have the answer! The eyes of the LORD are in every place beholding the evil and the good (Prov. 15:3, KJV). Yes, he looks upon the evil and recognizes its presence, yet he has set an appointed time to bring evil to a perpetual end. When sin entered the world so did evil.

> And God saw that the wickedness of man was great in the earth, and that every imagination of the thoughts of his heart was only evil continually. And it repented the LORD that he made man on the earth, and it grieved him at his heart. (Gen. 6:6–7, KJV)

Man of himself and by himself can do nothing about the evil that is within him or in the world. To question God or his existence as if he has a right to be answered is somewhat foolish. The scriptures have defined Satan as the evil one who has deceived the whole world is a liar, thief, and murderer. What can man of his own accord do to him? "For we wrestle not against flesh and blood, but against principalities, against powers, against the rulers of darkness of this world, against spiritual wickedness in high places" (Eph. 6:12, KJV). The reality is we are truly like sheep fragile, no defense system, stupid and may I say ignorant, we are but bait for the taking captive at the will of the enemy. Sheep do not hear or see well, by nature. they are just dumb, fragile. and prone to go astray. I know this is not how we would naturally view ourselves but just consider how ill equipped we are in spiritual matters; in most cases, we deny the reality of them. Because of the nature and character of sin in man, it has dominion over the flesh rendering him spiritually dead. But I see another law in my members, warring against the law of my mind, and bringing me into captivity to the law of sin, which is in my members. "O wretched men that I am! Who shall deliver me from the body of this death?" (Rom. 6:23–24, KJV). This is the tragedy that we are faced with because of sin and the presence of evil and it cannot be denied. Sin is greater than any man or religion is able to contend with. The darkness and death that it produces has reign from Adam until this present hour. There is no escape that man can create or no strength that man can produce to deliver from its grip. Sin has deceived man and destroyed him spiritually beyond repair that is why man must be born again.

Spiritual argument: To be spiritually dead makes one unaware of the reality of spiritual things, there is no capacity to discern, comprehend, or even desire. This is not a matter of opinion but of spiritual reality. "Verily, verily, I say unto thee, except a man is born again, he cannot see the kingdom of God" (John 3:3, KJV). Just imagine for a moment that you know, that you know, that you do not know God. You do not have any real understanding about the reality of his person, and even if you question his existence, it doesn't negate the possibility that he is, and you are ignorant of the fact. That being said, understand this, it is God who has said that man is spiritually dead and that you must be again. Spiritual death was the result of Adam's disobedience, in the beginning when God made known his judgment, that if he ate of the tree of the knowledge of good and evil, that in that day he would "surely die." We are the ones in need of his help not the opposite; he does not need our help. "For what man knoweth the things of a man, save the spirit of man which is in him? Even so the things of God knoweth no man, but the Spirit of God" (1 Cor. 2:11, KJV). Our attention is not naturally on the things of God because we are not inclining to desire them. One of the most significant challenges that we must face is the realization of our spiritual death and the consequences thereof. Spiritual death literally is to be alienated from the life of God in this world. God has declared that we do not know him, do not understand him or truth, do not desire him, and do not even seek him. How then can any men in his own mind attribute any credibility to his own thought or assessment of God. At best, he must acknowledge his ignorance and proceed with caution on all of his presumptions and imaginations. Spiritual life and understanding comes from the Only True and Living God, and he is liberal to all those who seek him in sincerity and truth.

It is important to note here that with 7.12 billion people on the face of the earth, spiritual death and darkness has made many sincerely wrong and believe lies. God is the one that determines how he is to be approached and the way he is to be approached, no man has that ability. Jesus said,

> Enter ye in at the strait gate: for wide is the gate, and broad is the way, that leadeth to destruction, and many there be I which go in there at: Because strait is the gate, and narrow is the way, which leadeth unto life, and few there be that find it. (Matt. 7:13–14, KJV)

Throughout the history of humanity, countless lies and misrepresentation of God has entered into the thoughts and imaginations of man. Cultures and entire civilizations have been apprehended by strong delusions about God. Man has constantly been guilty of calling evil good and good evil. Substituting darkness for light and light for darkness, and putting bitter for sweet and sweet for bitter. Because that, when they knew God, they glorified him not as God, neither were thankful; but became vain in their imaginations, and their foolish heart was darkened. Professing themselves to be wise, they became fools and changed the glory of God into an image made like corruptible man, and birds, and four-footed beast, and creeping things (Rom. 1:21–23, KJV). Consider your own thoughts and imaginations about God, where do they originate from and what the source of their validity is. Many will say that man wrote the Bible, and it has been translated so much that it is hard to believe what is truth or myth. This would be a good argument if God was not able to preserve truth from generation to generation, seeing that it is his responsibility to make it known, not men. Here is a caution for all to consider and take heed too; it is a privilege to be able now to come into the knowledge of spiritual truth. No one has any rights or personal claims that they can magnify or justify to man or God about knowing what is spiritual truth. God has chosen by his grace and mercy to be willing to allow man to come into the knowledge of the truth on his terms alone. God is not indebted to man, but those that have been translated from darkness into his marvelous light and are now his ambassadors, are to become such. The apostle Paul alter coming into the knowledge of the truth said,

> I am debtor both to the Greeks, and to the Barbarians, both to the wise, and to the unwise... For I am not ashamed of the gospel of Christ: for it is the power of God unto salvation to everyone that believeth: to the Jew first, and also to the Greek. For therein is the righteousness of God revealed from faith to faith: as it is written the just shall live by faith. (Rom. 1:14, 16–17, KJV)

Spiritual truth has been declared by the righteousness of God, and he has made that truth known through the gospel (good news) of Christ. You can now come to know the True and Living God and Jesus Christ with spiritual understanding that surpasses all others if you seek him by faith with your whole heart diligently. God is a jealous God, and he has set a high value on the knowledge of God, and that value was the death of his Son. He died so that you could have an opportunity to come to know him in the truth.

Jesus said, "That which is born of the flesh is flesh; and that which is born of the Spirit is spirit. Marvel not that I said unto thee, Ye must be born again" (John 3:6–7, KJV). There is a notable difference between that which is natural and that which is spiritual. The sad reality is that the natural-minded man is not subject to the things of God, and it is impossible for him to be so because they are spiritual. It is imperative to make spiritually alive, but one must come to the realization that they are spiritually dead before this can happen. If you do not recognize a need, then why would you even consider it as a problem? There can be no confusion when it comes to the matters of spiritual truth, either you have spiritual life or you don't, either you have spiritual understanding or you don't. There is life and peace in the mind and hearts of those who know and understand the freedom and liberty of being made spiritually alive. Likewise, there is a continual bondage and spiritual darkness that binds one in spiritual death because of sin that can only be delivered from by spiritual power from God alone. God has made that power known and available in the gospel of his dear Son the Lord Jesus Christ, therefore in Christ stead; (as if God himself was begging you) I beseech you to be reconciled to God! Do not deprive yourself of the wonderful privilege to come to know the True and Living God and Jesus Christ.

15

The God of Faith

But without faith it is impossible to please him:
for he that cometh to God must believe that he is,
and that he is a rewarder of them that diligently
seek him.

—Hebrews 11:6 (KJV)

There is no one like God; he alone is holy, omnipotent, omniscient, and omnipresent. No one has seen him at any time, and no man can approach him. He is self-existing and without him, nothing would be because by him all things consist. There is none that can be compared unto him and no other god beside him, for he is God alone. Who is this God? What is he about? Why is he so mysterious? These are curious questions that should be considered normal to the natural-minded man, questions that should be investigated. I previously stated that there are a variety of belief systems that has influenced mankind from generation to generation. How we believe is just as important as what we believe. For example, it takes a great sense of faith to believe that an explosion in the galaxy would formulate the universe, place a microorganism in water that would become a tadpole-like lifeforms that would come out of the water and become an ape, then become a man and saturate the earth. It would take even greater faith to believe that man could be born of a woman and live only to die, and then choose what lifeform that he could come back as in another life. These things may seem somewhat comical or far reaching with sarcasm; however, they resemble some of the belief systems that man has embraced with wholehearted devotion. The God of the Bible has made himself known with many infallible proofs recorded in his word that he has used to reveal himself, and the work of his hands, throughout the history of our known existence. These words are a testimony to his person and integrity and also an accurate accounting of who he is, what he is about, and also the revelation of the mystery of God. These words also unveil a covenant, which he has established and maintained with man from the beginning of creation until this present hour. It is the hope and expectation of these words that make God, the God of faith, for faith is only connected to what he has said. "So then faith cometh by hearing, and hearing by the word of God" (Rom. 10:17, KJV).

To begin to understand anything that God has made known about himself, we must have our hearing aligned with his speaking. It is easy for us to assume and prejudge God and the things that he has spoken because by nature, we are full of our own prejudices. It is also a known fact that many have open the pages of scripture and either found themselves confused about what they were reading due to a lack of understanding, or they have read into scripture something that was not implied due to a lack of understanding. We all have in one way or another formulated some thoughts and/or opinions about God, what he has said, what he has done, or what he has not done. We take it upon ourselves to scrutinize the God of heaven and earth as if we have the ability to make good judgment concerning him and his things. Jesus said, "If any man has ears to hear, let him hear. And he said, take heed what ye hear: with what measure ye mete, it shall be measured to you: and unto you that hear shall more be given" (Mark 4:23–24, KJV). How we fail to take the word of God and value it for its true worth, it is in itself the very foundation of the source of faith in God. If it is impossible for God to lie if he has made known to us excellent counsel and knowledge about the words of truth, then we should be able to trust in it. What God has said and calls upon us to believe, we should in return boldly say what he has said, trusting only in him to honor his word. He is the God of faith, because he wrote the words that faith are built upon. He has chosen words to be the medium wherein he made known truth and ordained them to be the substance of things hoped for. It is his words that are declared to be spirit and life and full of exceeding great and precious promises. It is upon the promises of the word of God that our hope and expectations rest. Even as he has admonished us to be, "Looking unto Jesus the author and finisher of our faith; who for the joy that was set before him endured the cross, despising the shame, and is set down at the right hand of the throne of God" (Heb. 11:2, KJV).

There is such a misunderstanding in regards to faith today because many just equate faith with just believing something.

> Yea, a man may say, thou hast faith, and I have works: shew me thy faith without works, and I will shew thee my faith by my works. Thou believe that there is one God; thou doest well: the devils believe, and tremble. But wilt thou know, O vain man, that faith without works is dead? (James 2:18–20, KJV)

The devil and demons believe in God, but that does not constitute faith although they are fully persuaded that he is God alone. Likewise, many men have proclaimed their faith in God, but it has not necessarily qualified as the biblical characterization of the faith designed by the God of faith. Jesus himself is the author of the faith that is grounded and rooted in what God has said. The objective of that faith is obedience to the True and Living God that leads to an intimate relationship with his person. It is what Jesus accomplished in his death on the cross and resurrection from the dead that laid the foundation for the faith that is connected directly to the God of faith. Therefore, to understand what God has said in regards to faith eliminates all presumptions about him and what actually constitutes biblical faith. This type of faith is great according to the scriptures, "And the Lord said, If ye had faith as a grain of mustard seed, ye might say unto this sycamine tree, Be thou plucked up by the root, and be thou planted in the sea; and it should obey you" (Luke 17:6, KJV). If we were to examine the character of biblical faith, we will see clearly that it is connected to the power of God and it is able to great things. The faith that the Bible produces creates a strong confidence in its objective who is God. This faith is also a specific faith; it rests entirely in the plan of redemption, which describes man's need for a Savior to deliver him from his deprived state of sin. Jesus alone, being the author of this faith written in his blood covenant for eternal life, gives it substance.

The God of faith has so designed faith to be built upon promises that he himself has made with evidence that he alone could provide. Wherein God, willing more abundantly to shew the heirs of promise the immutability of his counsel, confirmed it by an oath. That by two immutable things, in which it was impossible for God to lie, we might have strong consolation, who have fled for refuge to lay hold upon the hope set before us (Heb. 6:17–18, KJV). God places himself as the only one responsible to uphold, validate, and manifest the promises of his word to those that believe. Men may make oaths and swear to God to profess their commitment of truth and allegiance, but God is not like man. There is no one greater than him so he holds himself accountable to those that trust his words by himself. His confirmation of his faithfulness is so sure that he has made Jesus Christ himself the anchor of its solidarity. Nothing can be more secure that the witness of one who desires to prove so great a love that they would die for you. The God of faith calls those to believe to count things that are not, as if they were, to look beyond that which is seen to view the unseen. To all who have no knowledge of the God of faith, he declares of himself as a witness even against himself on their behalf that it is impossible for him to lie. For him to lie would discredit all that he stands for, for him to lie would be against his very existence because he is eternal truth. There is no ability within him to waver in any direction to the right or left. He is steadfast, unmovable, and forever consistent with all truth, the whole truth, and nothing but the truth. Now faith is the substance of things hoped for, the evidence of things not seen (Heb. 11:1, KJV). The

God of faith has chosen faith as the means whereby all men can come to know him through his word.

The word of God has been the object of the attacks of Satan himself from the beginning of creation to hinder man from being established in Truth. As you will recall, it was the very words, "Hath God said that was boldly uttered to create doubt and a questioning spirit that was against God." God did not have a need to prove that what he had said was true because of who he is. But it was this subtle intrusion into the mind and heart of man that deprived him of the most important characteristic that man would need to relate with the God of faith, which was faith. Doubt and faith cannot coexist for it is likened unto light and darkness, or even life and death. We can clearly see that faith in the word of God was required in the beginning and since God is the God of faith who changeth not, neither has his means. The God of faith takes note of faith in its very essence as most pleasing to his person as it represents the highest respect and admiration toward him. When Jesus was confronted by a woman from Canaan who desire him to heal her daughter, he said:

> I am not sent but unto the lost sheep of the house of Israel. Then came she and worshipped him, saying, Lord, help me. But he answered and said, it is not meet to take the children's bread, and to cast it to dogs. And she said, Truth, Lord: yet the dogs eat of the crumbs which fall from their masters" table. Then Jesus answered and said unto her, O woman, great is thy faith: be it unto thee even as thou wilt. And her daughter was made whole from that very hour. (Matt. 15:24–28, KJV)

The God of faith recognizes that faith is directly related to truth about who he is and what he has said. This is fascinating; to comprehend the value that God has attached to faith in his word because his word represents who he is, and it is impossible for him to lie.

Whatever may come to oppose the truth of the word of God, true faith stands the test of enduring all that would resist the truth. Herein is the connection: "In the beginning was the Word, and the Word was with God, and the Word was God" (John 1:1, KJV). The God of faith is not only faithful and true to his word, he is in fact one with his Word. Man in his low estate and spiritual ignorance have no idea of the wonderful grace that God has made known unto him through his word. God not only so loved the world that he gave his only begotten Son, he has positioned himself to give us himself. He said to Abraham who was a type of father of the faith because he believed God, "Fear not Abram: I am thy shield and thy exceeding great reward" (Gen. 15:1, KJV). Abraham would receive the testimony of being the friend of God. How can we neglect the awesomeness of the fact that God has chosen to give himself to us. If you could just imagine what it was like before sin entered the world. The fellowship between God, Adam, and Eve must have been sweet for the moment. There was no concern about right and wrong, good or evil. There was no need for God to provide a covering for them to hide their nakedness. Death did not exist, both did; time for God was with them and his presence was the fullness of joy. With much difficulty, we can vaguely imagine the potential perfect peace and pleasure of the state of innocence. The God of faith has no difficulty reviewing the reality of it. He purposed it to be, and it is his desire to reclaim that which is rightly his. He is jealous for you, seeing that sin and many other things have deprived him from being able to give himself to you, and you not being able to sense it.

Faith has been a questionable concern for many who have been more convinced of the ability of man through scientific research and analysis to validate and draw conclusions about data. However, there is no data or research that can be used to compare or evaluate God.

> Thus saith the LORD, thy redeemer, and he
> that formed thee from the womb. I am the LORD
> that maketh all things; that stretcheth forth the
> heavens alone; that spreadeth abroad the earth
> by myself; That frustrateth the tokens of liars,

and maketh diviners mad; that turneth wise men
backward, and maketh their knowledge foolish.
(Isa. 44:24–25, KJV)

The God of faith has made himself known and the counsel of
his will and that without reservation. He does not depend on fiction
because of the demands or assessments of men. How we view God
affects every aspect of our life. Many view God as great and all powerful but not really concerned or involved with the day-to-day issues
of their life. Many see God as someone afar off in heaven waiting on
us to die so we can see what is next. Others view him in the scope
of their particular religious beliefs or their unbelief, but the God of
faith is only to be viewed from his perspective how he has revealed
himself. In the scriptures from Genesis to Revelation is the complete
thought of the will and person of God. By faith, look unto me and
seek me diligently and you shall find me. By faith, understand the
things that I have done from the beginning of creation until the end
of this world. Through faith, I have designed a plan of redemption to
reconcile you unto myself and deliver you from the sin and darkness
that is against you. Through faith, you can be forgiven of all of your
sins and made whole and become a child of God, inheriting all the
claims and rights bestowed through being eternally adopted.

The God of faith is the Only Wise God, and he alone in the
multitude of his tender mercies has done all that is needed to make
himself known.

> These words spake Jesus, and lifted up
> his eyes to heaven, and said, Father, the hour is
> come; glorify thy Son, that thy Son also may glo-
> rify thee: As thou hast given him power over all
> flesh, that he should give eternal; life to as many
> as thou hast given him. And this is life eternal,
> that they might know thee the only true God,
> and Jesus Christ, whom thou hast sent. (John
> 17:1–3, KJV)

God is the God of truth, and he is absolute about all men coming into the knowledge the truth about him. You could say that he is jealous for you to come to know him in the truth only because you do not know him. There are so many thoughts that could be thought, so many lies that could and are being promoted, but there is only one truth about who God is! He desires to be known, and he desires that you come to know him for who he is and as he is. There is nothing that can compare to coming to know the True and Living God. There is no knowledge that meets the spirit of excellence like the knowledge of God. The knowledge of God has been valued from all those that know him as priceless. The apostle Paul said:

> But what things were gains to me, those I counted loss for Christ. Yea doubtless, and I count all things but loss for the excellency of the knowledge of Christ Jesus my Lord: for whom I have suffered the loss of all things, and do count them but dung that I may win Christ. (Phil. 3:17–8, KJV)

No one has ever gone to the extent to make themselves known like the God of heaven and earth has. No one has desired to be known in the truth with such passion that it could be said, "I am jealous that you would not want to know me, considering who I am!" Could you imagine that he that formed you in your mother's womb, cares so much about you having an opportunity to come to know him that he would say:

> I will put my laws into their mind and write them in their hearts: and I will be to them a God, and they shall be to me a people; And they shall not teach everyman his neighbor, and every man his brother, saying, Know the Lord: for all shall know me, from the least to the greatest. For I will be merciful to their unrighteousness, and their sins and iniquities will I remember no more. (Heb. 8:10b-13, KJV)

Oh! Those men would come to view God as he has made himself known. The God of faith is the God of the Bible! He is the God who has chosen words to make himself known by, and he has magnified his word above his name. The word of God is the substance of the faith that the God of faith has declared, and it is the evidence that he has determined to be sufficient for all things pertaining to life and godliness for his name sake.

Conclusion

What Must This Man Do To?

And he said, Sirs, What must I do to be saved?
And they said, Believe on the Lord Jesus Christ
and thou shalt be saved, and thy house.

—Acts 16:30–31 (KJV)

It has been said often times, "What you don't know won't hurt you," but I boldly proclaim to you, that is a lie from the depths of hell. Ignorance has been one of man's greatest enemies and to this day, it still is. Ignorance isn't bliss; it is dangerous and foolish to all that it has in its grips. No! It is not better for you to be ignorant of all the facts that pertain unto life and death. No! It does make a difference in what you believe and the validity of its worth. No! You do not have to die and go to hell because of your sinfulness. God is the God of all knowledge and he said, "My people are destroyed for lack of knowledge" (Hos. 4:6, KJV), and again, "Have not I written to thee excellent things in counsels and A knowledge, that I might make thee know the certainty of the words of truth; that thou mightiest answer the words of truth to them that send unto thee?" (Prov. 22:20–21, KJV). It is not the will of God for man to be ignorant, especially when it pertains to knowing the truth about him. He beckons man to come seek to know and understand for his glory and their good. He also warns man of the consequences of their failure to desire to know.

How long, ye simple ones, will ye love simplicity? And the scorners delight in their seeming and fools hate knowledge? Turn you at my reproof: behold, I will pour out my spirit unto you, I will make known my words unto you. Because I have called, and you refused; I have stretched out my hand, and no man regarded; I also will laugh at your calamity; I will mock when your fear cometh; when your fear cometh as desolation, and your destruction cometh as a whirlwind; when distress and anguish cometh upon you. Then shall they call upon me, but I will not answer; they shall seek me early, but they shall not find me: For that they hated knowledge, and did not choose the fear of the Lord. They would none of my counsel: they despised all my reproof. (Prov. 1:22–30, KJV)

It is upon the foundation of these scripture that I would challenge you to consider carefully what you must do. After all that has been said in reference to God being jealous for you because of his image, his will, and his glory, I would conclude with the thought that, there must be a need for respect.

Respect for who he is, his judgments, and all his counsel. Respect for what he has purposed in his heart before the foundation of the world, in the magnificent work of redemption. Respect shows forth the admiration, esteem, honor, and reverence that is due to him for he alone is worthy. We have shown and given respect to our parents, teachers, and governing officials from police officers, judges, politicians, and even the president. How is it that we can show even the smallest inclination of respect for these and absolutely none for the creator of heaven and earth, and all that therein are. I will use the word *respect* in an acronym to validate what you must do—that will certainly bring glory and honor to God—but also bless you exceedingly, abundantly, above that which you could even ask or think.

Let's start with the letter R, is for *repent*. In this day and age, we find that the word repent has seemed to have lost its effectiveness because we are too easily moved by pleasing man and our concern for pleasing God has been devalued. God do not require repentance, he demands it.

> And the times of this ignorance God winked at but now commandeth that all men everywhere to repent. Because he hath appointed a day, in which he will judge the world in righteousness by that man whom he hath ordained; whereof he hath given assurance to all men, in that he hath raised him from the dead. (Acts 17:30–31, KJV)

Repentance is needed to create in man the right spirit of mind and will toward responding to God. We live in a day where we are offering anything to God and think that it is acceptable, we are worshipping him with our mouths, but our hearts are far from him. True repentance has specific characteristics that need to be understood and manifested. Repentance must originate from godly sorrow not self-pity, it must create within us a desire to clear ourselves with God. We will have a genuine desire for him and his things as we return to him with the right spirit of repentance. Repentance becomes a part of our disposition and establishes us in the fear of the Lord that we no longer love sin, but we hate it. Lastly, true repentance creates within us a zeal for God to resist sin, the world, and the devil. Howbeit the process of manifesting godly sorrow that leads to repentance may be progressive it is sure and built upon the word of God not feelings and emotions.

> Repent ye therefore, and be converted, that your sins may be blotted out, when the times of refreshing shall come from the presence of the Lord; and he shall send Jesus Christ, which before was preached unto you. Whom the heaven must receive until the times of restitution of all things, which God hath spoken by the mouth of all his holy prophets since the world began. (Acts 3:19–21, KJV)

The first E is for *escape*. Why escape? We need to be reminded that God is Holy, and he was offended by the act and presence of sin. In understanding the gross nature of the offense, you will also understand the wrath of God, and it is his wrath that we need to escape from. God is saving us by himself, for himself, from himself! "For the wrath of God is revealed from heaven against all ungodliness and unrighteousness of men, who hold the truth in unrighteousness" (Rom. 1:18, KJV). God is justified in expressing his anger because he is Omnipotent, Omniscient, and Omnipresent; there is no other God! He is holy, just and pure; he is light and in him is no darkness at all, he alone is righteous. There is the necessity to break free from the sin and bondage that entangles, break free from the pending judgment to come. "It is appointed unto men once to die, but after this the judgment" (Heb. 9:27, KJV). Regardless of what belief system man may find himself persuaded by, he will still have to face death whether he believed it or not. It is the reality of what happens after death that should be the utmost concern. If what the Bible describes is true, then the warnings that it convey are for man to escape. The level of eternal damnation and destruction is never-ending torment that supersedes the imagination and warrants wailing and gnashing of teeth. Escape! Is the admonition of the scriptures for who is able to stand before his wrath. It would be better to take advantage of the riches of his grace and loving-kindness that he has shown, than to do despite to his grace and meet his wrath. Another aspect that should not be overlooked is, "How, shall we escape if we neglect so great salvation; which at the first began to be spoken by the Lord, and was confirmed unto us by them that heard him" (Heb. 2:3, KJV). The admonishment is to escape, but herein is a strong warning also within the question; that suggest that if we refuse to take the escape route that God has provided through the great plan of salvation, that *there will be no escape* from the wrath of God. Again, God is not willing that any should perish but, that all men everywhere repent and believe the gospel that they might be saved. But if they refuse to respond to his grace and mercy on their own accord, he warns of the consequences. See that ye refuse not him that speaketh. For if they escaped not who refuseth him that spake on earth, (referring to the fact that those that despised the law given by Moses died without mercy under two or three witnesses: "Of how much sorer punishment suppose ye, shall be thought worthy, who hath trodden underfoot the Son of God, and hath counted the blood of the covenant, wherewith he was sanctified, an unholy thing, and hath done despite unto the spirit of grace" (Heb. 10:28–29, KJV)? much more shall not we escape if we turn away from him that speaketh from heaven.

S is for *seek*. We learned earlier that God had judged that there was none that seeketh after God, no not one. This is such a horrible state to be in when there is so much that God desires to make known unto us. What is involved in the process of seeking? I like to liken seeking to exercise; it is an exercising of the senses to come to a desired end. It involves activity to improve upon that which is lacking. The objective of seeking is to come to know and understand, to find out knowledge and in this case, the knowledge of God. The scriptures declare that:

> Yea, if thou criest after knowledge, and liftest up thy voice for understanding; If thou seekest her as silver, and searchest for her as for hid treasure; Then shalt thou understand the fear of the LORD, and find the knowledge of God. (Prov. 2:3–5, KJV)

This scripture is fundamental and imperative to any genuine desire to come to know God. God not only tells us that he desires that we should seek him; he gives us specific insight into how to seek him so that we will find him. One of the most dangerous things anyone could do to hinder them in their pursuit of God is to fail to do what he said, how he said it. Notice here his detailed instructions in seeking—first there is the need to cry, yes cry! When a baby senses within itself the desire for food, attention, or anything that is making them uncomfortable that demands attention, the only thing they can do is cry. They do not have the ability to help themselves, they do not understand, they are totally dependent; therefore, they cry out for help. It is this strong overbearing desire that something must be done now to help me that they are making known. Likewise, we really need to see the urgent need for a desire for help that would cause us to cry out to God in sincerity and truth. Ye must be born again then. "As newborn babes, desire the sincere milk of the word that ye may grow" (1 Pet. 2:2, KJV).

Second, we must value the word and knowledge of God comparably like searching for a treasure that is hidden. This is not a natural desire that we have, but the desire that God desires that you have. It should cause you to cry out to him to create within us such a desire. The knowledge of God should be viewed as something of great worth and esteemed as rare and precious because of the nature of it. David said, "I love thy commandments above gold; yea, above fine gold" (Ps. 119:127, KJV). We can learn much from David seeing that God gave him the testimony of being a man after his heart, and it was because of his passion for the word of God. His view of God was defined only by what God said of himself, it is this view of God that brings glory and honor to his name. Third and I think most importantly, the need to have an understanding and inclination toward the fear of the Lord. In today's society, culture, and even among believers, there is missing a sense of awe, wonder, and adoration of the True and Living God that has an inherent respect toward his person, all of his thoughts, and all of his judgments. This assessment is the framework for the foundation of the fear of the Lord. His very existence should bring to our conscience an awareness of his exalted majesty and glory that causes us to bow down on our knees and worship him. For he is the only wise God, he alone is holy, perfect in wisdom, knowledge, and understanding. He is omnipotent, omniscient, and omnipresent! "Let all the earth fear the Lord: let all the inhabitants of the world stand in awe of him" (Ps. 33:8, KJV). The Bible speaks expressively about the fear of the lord and the benefits of it He is to be feared above all others with an accurate understanding of it. Finally, he concludes that with these components in their perspective places with application the promise of assurance is implemented, you shall find the knowledge of God!

P is for *pray*. Oftentimes, when we are at our wit's end, we will utter a prayer quickly unto the Lord requesting his immediate attention, with a sense of urgency for help. Now, rather or not, that we really have faith to believe that he will answer is another question. But at this moment in this presentation, I would like to convey a few thoughts on the subject of prayer. "And he spake a parable unto them to this end, that men ought always to pray, and not faint" (Luke 18:1, KJV). What is prayer? There are countless examples of prayers in the scriptures but what do they convey to us. Prayer assumes that *God is listening and is concerned about what you have to say.* When we engage in any communication with another, it is reasonable to expect the listener to pay attention and respond accordingly. Prayer is the means of communication that God has established for us to relate with him. Within the framework of prayer is confession, supplications, petitions, request, praise, worship, meditation, and intercession and what is God listening for when we pray? What causes God to respond to what we might say? "If my people, which are called by my name, shall humble themselves, and pray, and seek my face, and turn from their wicked ways; then will I hear from heaven, and will forgive their sin, and will heal their land" (2 Chron. 7:14, KJV). God has a prerequisite for prayer, and he takes notice of specific behavior. His grounds for the right attitude of prayer are for one to humble themselves. God hates pride; therefore, he does not respond to the proud, but his ears are open to the humble. It is the childlike spirit that gets the attention of God; those that are broken and contrite arouse his senses. We must understand that God will always resist the arrogant and stiff-necked, but more grace is reserved for the poor and needy. In the Old Testament as well as the New Testament, there are great examples of the right spirit of prayer that has been recorded for our admonition. We can sense the sincerity and truth of their humility and dependence upon God.

> And at the evening sacrifice I arose up from
> my heaviness; and having rent my garment and
> my mantle, I fell upon my knees, and spread out
> my hands unto the LORD my God, And said,
> O my God I am ashamed and blush to lift up
> my face to thee, My God: for our iniquities are

increased over our head and our trespass is grown up to the heavens. (Ezra 9:5–6, KJV)

Another example that is consistent with this same spirit of truth we find in the New Testament writings.

Two men went up into the temple to pray; the one a Pharisee, and the other a publican. The Pharisee stood and prayed thus within himself, God, I thank thee, that I am not as other men are, extortionist, unjust, adulterers, or even as this publican. I fast twice in the week; I give tithes of all that I possess. And the publican, standing afar off, would not lift up so much as his eyes unto heaven, but smote his breast, saying, God be merciful to me a sinner. I tell you, this man went down to his house justified rather than the other: for every one that exalteth himself shall be abased; and he that humbleth himself shall be exalted. (Luke 18:10–14, KJV)

Prayer is not just closing our eyes and uttering words to an invisible God who we cannot see. It is a mandatory necessity of humbling oneself under the mighty hand of God and crying out to him for mercy in all things that pertain to him. We must pray confessing our sinfulness to him, beseeching him for forgiveness that we might be made right with him. We must pray to set our hearts and minds right with him in prayer to carefully meditate upon the truth of his word. We must pray to make known to him the praises due to his name for his amazing grace and tender mercies. We must pray believing and confessing that Jesus Christ died for our sins, was buried and rose from the grave the third day according to the scriptures. "For with the heart man believeth unto righteousness; with the mouth confession is made unto salvation. For the scripture saith, whosoever believeth on him shall not be ashamed" (Rom. 10:10–11, KJV). Prayer is the conduit that aligns the spirit of man with the spirit of God when he approaches him on his term in his designated way. For the God of faith is God alone, who only hath immortality dwelling in the light which no man can approach unto: "To whom he honour and power everlasting. Amen" (1 Tim. 6:16, KJV). Therefore, men must pray and not faint, for his ears are open to them that call upon him in sincerity and truth.

The second E is for *examining*. If I could convince anyone of anything, it would be to recognize the importance of having a good understanding so that they can be clear on a matter. The scriptures put it in this wise: "Wisdom is the principal thing: therefore get wisdom: and with all thy getting get understanding" (Prov. 4:7, KJV). To have the capacity to perceive and grasp insight with knowledge and good judgement requires examination. Many people fail to investigate thoroughly information or the knowledge of somethings so that you can know and determine the true nature of it. God is not like that; he exhorts us to seek, ask, and search out a matter that we may become fully persuaded of its validity. To be presumptuous from God's perspective is not only dangerous, it also will lead to sin. The word of God makes the declaration about itself to be a light to our path and a lamp to our feet. This is not mere coincidence for God is light and in him is no darkness at all. Light gives us the ability to see things clearer so that we can investigate them more closely. Jesus said that he is the light of the world.

> He that believeth on him is not condemned: but he that believeth not is condemned already, because he hath not believed in the name of the only begotten Son of God. And this is the condemnation, that light is come into the world, and men loved darkness rather than light, because their deeds were evil. For every one that doeth evil hateth the light, neither cometh to the light, lest his deeds should be reproved. But he that doeth truth cometh to the light, that his deeds may be made manifest, that they are wrought in God. (John 3:18–21, KJV)

Faith is not built upon ignorance; neither is God requiring man to blindly believe something that is not true like some old wives fable or mythology. He calls man to come to seek to know the truth in the light with a passion and desire to examine it and secure understanding.

To really examine things that God desire demands a spirit of diligence. Notice how serious God is about you coming to know and examine truth.

> And besides this, giving all diligence, add to your faith virtue, and to virtue knowledge; and to knowledge temperance; and to temperance patience; and to patience godliness; and to godliness brotherly kindness; and to brotherly kindness charity. For if these things be in you, and abound, they make you that ye shall neither be barren nor unfruitful in the knowledge of our Lord Jesus Christ. (2 Pet. 1:5–8, KJV)

God has presented himself and his things in such a fashion that make them not only worthy of examination, but they can only be discovered by careful examination. When you have a mind to examine something, it is for the purpose to find out more about it. No examination could be flippant or without having some detailed orientation. When it comes to God teaching about his knowledge, he does not take it lightly. Consider what he spoke concerning this, whom shall he teach knowledge? "Whom shall he make understand doctrine? Them that are weaned from milk, and drawn from the breast. For precept must be upon precept; line upon line, line upon line; here a little, and there a little" (Isa. 28:9–10, KJV). There is no reason that anyone could conclude that God does not want them to know him in the truth with good understanding because he not only want you to examine yourself, he also wants you to examine the faith.

The C is for *confess*. When we hear the word confess, we automatically assume it has something to do with us going behind a curtain and making some confession to a priest about the ills of our life of sin, or someone who has been caught or found to be guilty of a crime. That may be relevant in many regards, but in this case, this confession is the most important confession that anyone will ever make in life. It is no secret that countless number of people despises and rejects the Lord Jesus Christ. But the thoughts and convictions of man to do so will have no bearing on the truth.

> Wherefore God also hath highly exalted him, and given him a name, which is above every name: That at the name of Jesus every knee should bow, of things in heaven, and things in earth, and things under the earth; And that every tongue should confess that Jesus Christ is Lord, to the glory of God the Father. (Phil. 2:9–11, KJV)

There is no other truth, as important as this, on earth or established in heaven, that God would require man to admit and submit too. It behooves us to examine why this is so important to God and imperative for man. Nothing can be done against the truth; we can suppress it, misrepresent it, lie about it, deny it, but we cannot change the reality of it. The sovereignty of God is not subject to the wiles of men. He has predetermined according to foreknowledge of his will to send his Son to die for the sins of the whole world. It was not a mistake or dysfunctional action from the mind of God to analyze and conclude the best possible answer to correct the problem that man created when he chose to violate the directive of God.

> For the day of vengeance is in mine heart, and the year of my redeemed is come. And I looked, and there was none to help; and I wondered that there was none to uphold; therefore mine own arm brought salvation unto me; and my tiny, it upheld me. (Isa. 63:4–5, KJV)

The plan of redemption was paid for by the blood of Jesus Christ on the cross of Calvary. It is because of this fact God commands all men everywhere to bow the knee and confess that he is Lord.

To confess is to agree with God that what he has said and done, you are willing to align yourself with and surrender to all the claims thereof. The righteousness of God is to be exalted and magnified in the earth and in man. What he accomplished through the death, burial, and resurrection is great and greatly to be praised. Jesus Christ is the righteousness of God. He is just and the justifier of those that believe in the resurrection of the dead. He has forever made peace with God and man, satisfying the demands of his judgement and delivering man from the bondage of sin and death. His blood has eternally secured the right of adoption, making us acceptable in the beloved wherein now we are the children of God. Translated from the power of darkness never to return, being forgiven forever and established in the kingdom of God, blessed with every spiritual blessing possible in Christ Jesus.

> For it pleased the Father that in him should all fullness dwell; And having made peace through the blood of his cross, by him to reconcile all things unto himself; by him, I say, whether they be things in earth, or things in heaven. (Col. 1:19–20, KJV)

Therefore, it is imperative for man to confess that Jesus is Lord, to the glory of God now, willfully for if not, there will come a day that every knee will bow, and every tongue will confess.

T is for *transform*. To completely and thoroughly change the nature, behavior, thinking, character, and state of man is God's objective. Sin has totally destroyed and deprived man of absolutely everything that God intended for him. Man is so completely blind and deceived in darkness that he has no awareness of his state or need. That is why the scriptures proclaim that ye must be born again. There is not a need for just a change; it is greater than that, and the need is to have an exchange. If our eyes were open just long enough to get a glimpse of the damage that sin did, we would never be the same. Our eyes could not look on the damage without us being totally horrified to death. If God would say that it repents him that he had made man once he saw the exceeding wickedness and evil imagination of his heart. The operation of God in Christ accomplished just that. God was in Christ reconciling all things unto himself and at the same time creating something absolutely new.

> For the love of Christ constraineth us; because we thus judge, that if one died for all, then were all dead: And that he died for all, then were all dead: And that he died for all, that they which live should not henceforth live unto themselves, but unto him which died for them, and rose again. Wherefore henceforth know we no man after the flesh: yea, though we have known Christ after the flesh, know us him no more. Therefore, if any man be in Christ, he is a new creature: old things are passed away; behold all things are become new. (2 Cor. 5:14–17, KJV)

This is the foundation for the exchanged life; God has totally eradicated the old man by literally taking him to the cross in Christ and crucifying him. From God's perspective, he killed him rendering him dead never to rise again. But he did not leave it there. God created a new man in Christ, willing and able to always do the things that please the Father.

God has completed the work that would free man and enable him to bring the glory intended to God in the beginning. Now there is liberty to serve God without the bondage of sin. The question is, how do we come to know and live according to this wonderful work that God has done? Paul gives us the answer, recognizing all that God has purposed and accomplished in Christ, he concludes.

> I beseech you therefore, by the mercies of God, that ye present your bodies a living sacrifice, holy, acceptable unto God, which is your

reasonable service. And be not conformed to this
world: but be ye transformed by the renewing of
your mind that ye may prove what is that good,
and acceptable, and perfect will of God. (Rom.
12:1–2, KJV)

Get the understanding that you may know why and how to do
the things that God requires you to do. There is the need for instruction that is why God designed the purpose of discipleship. However,
it is difficult to impossible to have discipleship without relationship.
God's design is that we might have godly relationships within the
family of God that leads to discipleship. Being a disciple of the Lord
Jesus Christ is one who enters into a covenant relationship with him
to continually learn to know, trust, worship, and obeys him. Being a
disciple of Christ means that your life is no longer your own and that
you recognize that it has be brought with a price. Being a disciple of
Christ means that you are willing to pick up your cross and follow
him wherever he might lead.

Being a disciple of Christ today has been substituted for going
to church. However, to come to know Jesus Christ and be his disciple, the process has not changed.

Then Jesus said unto his disciples. If any
man will come after me, let him deny himself,
and take up his cross, and follow me. For whosoever will save his life shall lose it: and whosoever
will lose his life for my sake shall find it. For what
is a man profited, if he shall gain the whole world,
and lose his own soul? Or what shall a man give
in exchange for his soul? (Matt. 16:24–26, KJV)

God created man in his own image and when he breathes in
him the breath of life, he became a living soul. This living soul God
intended to be a representation of himself on earth as he is in heaven.
Unfortunately, sin distorted and destroyed that from happening. But
God is true to his word, what he had said in the beginning that "it

was very good." Although sin destroyed, God purposed to revive and recreate. Although sin caused all to be loss, God took it personal and sought to find. Although sin brought about death, God destroyed death and restored everlasting life. God is jealous for his image, his will, and his glory. For this purpose, God so loved the world that he gave his only begotten Son to redeem them. His image was distorted by man's disobedience; his will was hindered on earth because of the darkness that sin brought in the world. His glory was not manifested as he intended because God is light and in him is no darkness at all. There is no fellowship with light and darkness. But glory be to Most High God!

> But God hath chosen the foolish things of the world to confound the wise; and God hath chosen the weak things of the world to confound the things that are mighty; and base things of the world, and things which are despised, hath God chosen, yea, and things which are not, to bring to naught things that are: That no flesh should glory in his presence. But of him are ye in Christ Jesus, who of God is made unto us wisdom, and righteousness, and sanctification, and redemption: that, according as it is written He that glorieth, let him glory in the Lord. (1 Cor. 1:27–31, KJV)

The God of the Bible has declared that he is a jealous God, and he has proven himself to be jealous for you. The good news of the gospel is that he has satisfied his righteous judgement and took vengeance on all of his enemies while preserving his right as God alone. The image of God has been restored in Christ; he being the expressed image of his person. The will of God has been fulfilled when Christ, having it being written of him to do thy will, bowed his head and said, "It is finished." God has proven with many infallible proofs that he is a jealous God, and throughout the history of mankind, he has worked to also prove that he is jealous for you, because you are his will, being made in his image only for his glory. Now the host of heaven rejoices and proclaims the manifestation of his glory. "Thou art worthy, O Lord, to receive glory and honour and power: for thou hast created all things, and for thy pleasure they are and were created" (Rev. 6:4:11, KJV). What must this man do? RESPECT and humble yourselves under the mighty hand of God and watch and see what he will do for you.

About the Author

Sidney Brehon Melvin was born in Norfolk, Virginia, and at the early age of eight could sense a call of God upon his life as he had a genuine sense of awe and wonder about the reality of God, although he did not know him. His heart was tender toward God, but his life would experience the reality of sin before he came into the knowledge of the Lord Jesus Christ. As a young teenager, he fell under great conviction to go to a Billy Graham Crusade but himself unworthy to go in, for he thought God deserved to have someone better than him because of his personal guilt and shame from sin. A failed Army career would find him facing forty years in Leavenworth Military prison. He had but one prayer, "Lord, if you would allow no harm to come upon me, I will serve you all the days of my life." That prayer would be the springboard to lead him to a life of affection and devotion to the Lord Jesus Christ.

His commitment to Christ was that of childlike faith with sincerity and truth as he grasped the simplicity of the gospel message. He cofounded the Mercy Seat Prison Ministry and served with great zeal and passion for over twenty years. He has been keen on exhibiting the gifts of help, exhortation, preaching, teaching, and ministry. He graduated from Liberty University with a bachelor of science in religion, recognizing that man is mostly influenced by what he believes or not believe about God. For as a man thinketh so is he. His passion is fueled the most by the impact of Hebrews 11:33–39 highlighting the "and others," living the life of faith in the Only Wise God; with emphasis on those who believed God and obtain such a testimony that "the world was not worthy of them" (Heb. 11:38a). His life has never been the same after he learned to live life to please God, not man, or ourselves.